GLAD TO BE ME

Building Self-Esteem
In Yourself
And Others

Revised and Expanded Edition

edited by

Dov Peretz Elkins

Preface by Sidney B. Simon

GROWTH ASSOCIATES
Human Relations Publishers
P.O. Box 18429
Rochester, NY 14618-0429

For Hillel, Jonathan and Shira
Jamie, Jeremy and Yoni
with love

Dr. Dov Peretz Elkins is author and editor of sixteen books on theology, education, psychology and human development. He has lectured and facilitated training workshops in North America, Israel, the U.S.S.R., and Europe. Dr. Elkins is Senior Rabbi of The Park Synagogue, one of the largest Conservative synagogues in the world.

Growth Associates
Human Relations Publishers and Consultants
P.O. Box 18429
Rochester, N.Y. 14618-0429
(716) 244-1225

Preface

Dov Peretz Elkins has made a most valuable contribution to the "search for self." He has compiled some of the wisest quotations on what it means to know something about the question: Who Am I?

I can see students eagerly eating up the quotations and the wisdom. In the hands of a creative leader, these readings will supply endless hours of fascinating debate, inquiry and values clarification.

One last thing. I think I just may hang a copy on a chain in the bathroom for company to read. Well, for me to read. I put it on a chain, because I know for sure, someone will want to rip it off for their very own. It is that good.

DR. SIDNEY B. SIMON, PROFESSOR OF EDUCATION, UNIV. OF
MASSACHUSETTS, AUTHOR, *VALUES CLARIFICATION*

Contents

Acknowledgement is accorded the following authors and sources of publications with reference to poems and excerpts included in the book:

m I TOUCH THE EARTH, THE EARTH TOUCHES ME, copyright © 1972 by Hugh ther. Reprinted by permission of Doubleday Company, Inc. Originally published in 1970 the Real People Press.

m "Self-Acceptance" by Eugene C. McDon- Jr., M.D., Bert Kruger Smith, and Robert L. herland, Ph.D., copyright the Hogg Founda- for Mental Health, The University of Texas, 2. Understanding Mental Health (a compila- of articles), copyright D. Van Nostrand npany, Inc., 1965.

m Kopp, S., IF YOU MEET THE BUDDHA THE ROAD, KILL HIM! Palo Alto, Cali- ia: Science and Behavior Books, 1972.

m Satir, V. PEOPLEMAKING. Palo Alto, fornia Science and Behavior Books, 1972.

es A. Gold, from Clark E. Moustakas, FIND- ; YOURSELF, FINDING OTHERS © 1974. permission of Prentice-Hall, Inc., Englewood 's, New Jersey.

l R. Rogers, ON BECOMING A PERSON. ston: Houghton Mifflin Company, 1961). d by permission.

vard J. Clinebell, Jr., THE MENTAL ALTH MINISTRY OF THE LOCAL URCH, Abingdon Press, Nashville, Tennessee.

erpt from pp. 47-49 ON CARING by Milton veroff, Volume Forty-three of the World Per- ctive Series, edited by Ruth Nanda Anshen. yright © 1971 by Milton Mayeroff.

erpt from THE KNOWLEDGE OF MAN by tin Buber (Harper & Row, 1965).

erpt from pp. 232-3, "Personality Problems Personality Growth," by A. H. Maslow in E SELF, edited by Clark E. Moustakas. yright © 1956 by Clark E. Moustakas.

erpt from pp. 101, 179, MOTIVATION AND RSONALITY, 2nd Edition by Abraham H. low (Harper & Row, 1970).

ıde Steiner, Scripts People Live (New York: ve Press, 1974, pp. 116-117.

n THE ONE QUEST, Claudio Naranjo. yright © 1973 by Claudio Naranjo. Reprinted permission of The Sterling Lord Agency, Inc.

n In the Stillness Is the Dancing by Mark ;, S. J. Copyright © 1972 Argus Communi- ons, Niles, IL. Reprinted with permission.

n Jeffrey Schrank, TEACHING HUMAN NGS. Copyright © by the Beacon Press.

n HOW TO MAKE WINNING YOUR LIFE LE by D. S. Viscott. Used with the permis- of the author.

yright © 1973 by Jerry A. Greenwald. Re- printed by permission of Simon & Schuster, Inc.

Lou Benson, IMAGES, HEROES AND SELF-PERCEPTIONS: The Struggle For Identity— From Mask Wearing to Authenticity, © 1974, pp. 58-60, 74, 119-120, 356-357. Reprinted by permission of Prentice-Hall, Inc., Englewood Cliffs, New Jersey.

Clark E. Moustakas, THE SELF, EXPLORA- TIONS IN PERSONAL GROWTH, pp. 9-11. Copyright © Harper, Colophon Books, 1974.

Copyright © 1975 by Gay Bryant. Excerpted from HOW I LEARNED TO LIKE MYSELF by Gay Bryant and Bockris-Wylie, published by Warner Books, Inc.

From Joseph Stein, EFFECTIVE PERSONAL- ITY, Brooks/Cole Publishing Company.

From John V. Gilmore, THE PRODUCTIVE PERSONALITY, Albion Publishing Company.

From ENCOUNTERS WITH THE SELF by Don E. Hamachek. Copyright © 1971 by Holt, Rinehart and Winston, Inc. Reprinted by permis- sion of Holt, Rinehart and Winston.

From "Studies in Self-Esteem" by Stanley Coopersmith. Copyright © by W. H. Freeman and Company, Publishers.

From J. H. Brenneck and R. G. Amick, The Struggle for Significance. Copyright © 1975, Benziger Bruce & Glencoe, Inc. Used by permis- sion of the Macmillan Publishing Co., Inc.

Reprinted from Hasidism and Modern Man by Martin Buber, copyright 1958, by permission of the publisher Horizon Press, New York.

From E. E. Cummings, SIX NONLECTURES, copyright by Harvard University Press, 1953.

William W. Purkey, SELF-CONCEPT AND SCHOOL ACHIEVEMENT © 1970. Reprinted by permission of Prentice-Hall, Inc., Englewood Cliffs, New Jersey.

Reprinted from Why Am I Afraid to Love? by John Powell. Copyright 1967, 1972 by Argus Communications, Niles, IL. Used with permis- sion.

From M. Dale Baughman, EDUCATOR'S HANDBOOK OF STORIES, QUOTES & HU- MOR, copyright © Prentice-Hall, Inc., 1963. Used with permission.

From Abraham H. Maslow, "Self-Actualizing People," Symposium #1, VALUES IN PER- SONALITY RESEARCH. Copyright © by Grune & Stratton, Inc., 1950. Used with permission.

From THE HUMAN COMEDY, William Saro- yan. Copyright © by Harcourt Brace Jovanovich, 1971. Used with permission.

Every effort has been made to identify sources, and the publishers will appreciate being informed of inadvertant errrors in this re

Part *I*

LOVE YOURSELF!

1

Accept Yourself

I say that I accept the way I am, but do I
accept it so fully that I am willing to act
on it—to actually *act* the way I am?

The paradox of progress is that I grow each
time I realize that I can only be where I am.

HUGH PRATHER

High self-esteem results from coming to terms with yourself
somewhere between your ambitions and your limitations.

LEE SAUL DUSHOFF

Before, I thought I was actually fighting for my own self-worth; that is why I so desperately wanted people to like me. I thought their liking me was a comment on me, but it was a comment on them.

HUGH PRATHER

Some Characteristics of a Self-Accepting Person

The self-accepting person is a participant in life rather than a spectator.

He is inclined to be objective, spontaneous, and emotionally and intellectually honest.

He tries to understand the interpersonal and environmental problems he faces, but he also accepts his limitations in gaining true insight concerning them.

He works out the best adjustment to life of which he is capable, often without fully understanding all that is involved.

However, he is willing to experience the pleasures and discomforts of self-revelation: i.e., he accepts the mixed pain and joy that accompany each change in his attitude and feeling toward himself and others.

His claims on life are, for the most part, reasonable. If he wants to be a member of the Country Club and yet cannot afford it, he finds other social and recreational outlets in keeping with his budget.

The self-accepting person without special talent or ability is able to share emotionally in the gifts of others without undue regret about his inborn deficiencies.

He does not brood about missed opportunities, lost causes, errors, and failures. Rather, he looks on them for what they can contribute to his doing things differently or better in the future.

He does not get stuck in the rut of irrational feelings of love, hate, envy, jealousy, suspicion, lust, and greed, because he lets each feeling spell out its special message for him.

Although the self-accepting person may prefer not to be alone or isolated from family or friends, yet, in special times, when aloneness or isolation is a necessity, he can endure lack of contact with his fellows.

The self-accepting person may or may not be conventional in his thinking, feeling, or behavior. But when he is unconventional, it is not for the purpose of flaunting convention but rather for the sake of expressing or fulfilling a valid personal or public need.

He is not rigidly guided by rules and moralisms; hence he is willing to alter values in keeping with new insights.

He grants to others their right to values not identical with his own.

The self-accepting person puts himself into life in terms of his highest insights. Yet he accepts the fact that, in its essence, it remains the mystery of mysteries.

E. C. MC DONALD, JR.

B. K. SMITH

R. L. SUTHERLAND

No one can make you feel inferior without your consent.

ELEANOR ROOSEVELT

Accept everything about yourself—I mean everything—not some things—everything. Every feeling, idea, hope, fear, smell, appearance—it is you and it is good. . . . You can do anything you choose to do; you can enjoy anything you choose to take part in, to be aware of. You are you and that is the beginning and the end—no apologies, no regrets—you are what you want —because you are you—and who can doubt that—who could want more—you have everything there possibly is—there is no more— you are everything—and you are so large and immense that you could never find the top or bottom—you will spend a lifetime enjoying the search—you will enjoy every minute—there is so much to know and experience within yourself.

JAMES A. GOLD

With smile, and subtle shift of position, they welcomed me into the ongoing dinner conversation. I tried hard to listen, I really did. But it was just the way it always was; I simply couldn't understand what they were saying. It was as if they spoke a foreign language. I never had learned to understand or to speak the social talk that everyone else seems to use as a way of getting along and being friendly.

I couldn't do it as a kid, and I can't do it now. That so very old, so terribly painful shyness was still there, and it still hurt just as much as it ever had. I was, of course, tempted to do my number of putting their whole thing down as superficial and with- out meaning. But I knew, as I always know, that the bewilderment and emptiness is [sic] at that moment mine, not theirs. . . .

That was when I finally got to it. This is just the way it was going to be . . . no matter what, I would always be as pain- fully shy and as bewildered by the social talk that brings people together, as shy and as bewildered as I had been since I was a kid. Without knowing what you say to leave without hurting, I pushed back my chair, stood up awkwardly, and silently wandered away.

When I awoke I knew, for the first time again, that . . . the shyness is mine, like it or not. It's the best of me and the worst of me, and only the covering it up, the hiding it, and the running from it is not me.

SHELDON KOPP

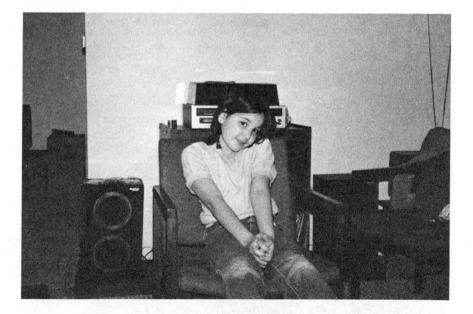

Do not worry about your difficulties in mathematics; I can assure you that mine are still greater.

ALBERT EINSTEIN

Over the piano was printed a notice: Please do not shoot the pianist. He is doing his best.

OSCAR WILDE

Do what you can, with what you have, with where you are.

THEODORE ROOSEVELT

Egg on My face

The comic characters of Chinese theater have a white triangular spot right over the nose. Its origin is an ancient joke about someone looking heavenward—and getting a bird dropping right on the face. To learn to carry that ignoble prize and make it something to grin about is an achievement.

We have all suffered when our inflated egos received an inevitable direct hit.

I had just finished delivering to a celebrated sports symposium what I considered to be one of my best lecture-demonstrations. My ego-balloon was soaring high. Then appeared a well-known New Age figure to entice me into one of his "new games," touted as joyful, noncompetitive mutual experiences.

With both of us intensely aware of our celebrity status before the assembled onlookers, we began tossing a raw egg back and forth as we gradually increased the distance between us. The game demands the ability to catch the egg gently, yielding with the impact so it will not break. The task becomes increasingly difficult as the distance is increased and the egg is thrown farther and higher. Sooner or later the egg has to break!

The showdown is that tense moment when you sense that the limit has been reached—the next catch is bound to be the last and you pray that the yolk will not be on you!

Of course, there is the choice of not trying to catch the egg, of simply letting it smash on the ground. But on that memorable day there was an audience egging us on. We had to continue trying the catch until—splat!

What a disrespectful mess! Egg all over the Tai Ji master's silk brocade jacket and on his conspicuous chagrin! Egg on my face and an unmistakable gleeful twinkle in my opponent's eye!

For several years the incident bothered me. It was a thorn in my ego. Now, finally, I have come to cherish that scene and its message about the value in risking egg on your face, literally and figuratively. Yes, I could have simply dodged the egg. Letting it fall would have saved face, not to mention the cleaning bill for my silk jacket. But what a meaningless story to tell!

I wear my white triangular spot with pride.

Maybe you have some symbolic bird-doo on your forehead or egg on your face. Pretending it isn't there only spreads the muck further. Display it and enjoy it. Turn it into a badge of honor.

AL HUANG

You grow up the day you have the first real laugh — at yourself.

ETHEL BARRYMORE

2

Trust Yourself

Still another way of describing this pattern which I see in each client is to say that increasingly he trusts and values the process which is himself. Watching my clients, I have come to a much better understanding of creative people. El Greco, for example, must have realized as he looked at some of his early work, that "good artists do not paint like that." But somehow he trusted his own experiencing of life, the process of himself, sufficiently that he could go on expressing his own unique perceptions. It was as though he could say, "Good artists do not paint like this, but *I* paint like this." Or to move to another field, Ernest Hemingway was surely aware that "good writers do not write like this." But fortunately he moved toward being Hemingway, being himself, rather that toward some one else's conception of a good writer. Einstein seems to have been unusually oblivious to the fact that good physicists did not think his kind of thoughts. Rather than drawing back because of his inadequate academic preparation in physics, he simply moved toward being Einstein, toward thinking his own thoughts, toward being as truly and deeply himself as he could. This is not a phenomenon which occurs only in the artist or the genius. Time and again in my clients, I have seen simple people become significant and creative in their own spheres, as they have developed more trust of the processes going on within themselves, and have dared to feel their own feelings, live by values which they discover within, and express themselves in their own unique ways.

CARL R. ROGERS

It is not always necessary to prove to others that one is right; it is sometimes enough to know it ourselves.

CHAIM GRADE

The best way I can state [the] aim of life, as I see it coming to light in my relationship with my clients, is to use the words of Soren Kierkegaard—"to be that self which one truly is."

I have little sympathy with the rather prevalent concept that man is basically irrational, and that his impulses, if not controlled, will lead to destruction of others and self. Man's behavior is exquisitely rational, moving with subtle and ordered complexity toward the goals his organism is endeavoring to achieve.

The individual increasingly comes to feel that this locus of evaluation lies within himself. Less and less does he look to others for approval or disapproval, for standards to live by, for decisions and choices. He recognizes that it rests within himself to choose; that the only question which matters is, "Am I living in a way which is deeply satisfying to me, and which truly expresses me?" This I think is perhaps *the* most important question for the creative individual.

CARL R. ROGERS

As soon as you trust yourself you will know how to live.

GOETHE

A person who doubts himself is like a man who would enlist in the ranks of his enemies and bear arms against himself. He makes his failure certain by himself being the first person to be convinced of it.

ALEXANDRE DUMAS

The late David Roberts once observed that if parents had to choose one thing which alone they could give their children, it should be a sturdy sense of their own worth. Without a solid sense of self-worth, a person is limited in his ability to live fully, to relate in a mutually fulfilling way, and to find a religious life with real depth. In Jean Anouilh's play "The Lark," the inquisitor declares in effect that the thing which made Joan of Arc dangerous was not that she had visions, but that *she had dared to trust in herself as a human being.*

HOWARD J. CLINEBELL, JR.

Self-trust is the first secret of success.

RALPH WALDO EMERSON

3

Affirm Yourself

The serious thing for each person to recognize vividly and poignantly, each for himself, is that every falling away from species-virtue, every crime against one's own nature, every evil act, *every one without exception records itself* in our unconscious and makes us despise ourselves. Karen Horney had a good word to describe this unconscious perceiving and remembering; she said it registers. And it registers *in our books!* If we do something we are ashamed of its registers to our discredit, and if we do something honest or fine or good it registers to our credit. The net results ultimately are either one or the other—either we respect and accept ourselves or we despise ourselves and feel contemptible, worthless, and unlovable. Theologians used to use the word *accidie* to describe the sin of failing to do with one's life all that one knows one can do.

ABRAHAM H. MASLOW

If I am not for myself, who will be?

ETHICS OF THE FATHERS, TALMUD

Let people realize clearly that every time they threaten someone or humiliate or hurt unnecessarily or dominate or reject another human being, they become forces for the creation of psychopathology, even if these be small forces. Let them recognize that every man who is kind, helpful, decent, psychologically democratic, affectionate, and warm, is a psychotherapeutic force even though a small one.

ABRAHAM H. MASLOW

Every person needs recognition. It is expressed cogently by the lad who says, "Mother, let's play darts. I'll throw the darts and you say 'Wonderful.' "

M. DALE BAUGHMAN

We can secure other people's approval, if we do right and try hard; but our own is worth a hundred of it.

MARK TWAIN

There is a great man who makes every man feel small. But the real great man is the man who makes every man feel great.

G. K. CHESTERTON

Stroking

Jack may find that he is not aware of many, if any, good things about himself and that he is incapable of using words which imply goodness or worth applied to him. If anyone attempts to supply strokes, he will reject some, most, or all of the strokes with a discount.

If someone says, "You have beautiful skin," the Parent says, internally, "They haven't seen you up close." If someone says, "You have a lovely smile," the Parent says, "But they haven't seen you angry." If a person says, "You're very intelligent," then the Parent says, "Yes, but you're ugly." Other devices to avoid the acceptance of strokes will be observed, such as: giving token acceptance of the stroke, followed by a shrug so that the stroke will roll off the shoulders instead of "soaking in"; or immediately reciprocating with a counter stroke which essentially says, "I don't deserve a stroke so I must give one in return." Another argument against taking strokes is, "These people don't know you, their strokes have got to be phony." This, in spite of the fact that everyone may have agreed to give only sincere, genuine strokes.

There are all sorts of taboos operating which prevent the free exchange of strokes: the homosexual taboo prevents stroking between men and men and women and women; the heterosexual taboo prevents stroking between men and women unless they are in a prescribed relationship, either engaged to be married or married; and certain taboos against physical touch prevent stroking between grownups and children unless they are part of a nuclear family, and then only under certain circumstances. In short, the free exchange of strokes is a managed activity, a situation in which the means of satisfaction of a basic need are made unavailable to people.

The end result is that the capacity to love is taken away from people and then directed against them by using it as a reinforcer to bring about desired behavior. . . .

Stroke satisfaction is the antidote to Lovelessness. . . .

CLAUDE STEINER

We may see in self-rejection what separates man from part of his experience, deprives him of the knowledge of what or who he is, creates conflicts, and takes away from the freedom to be himself in the surrendering to his own style and calling.

The rejection in the early years of life arrests the individual's growth, and the whole therapeutic process may be seen as one of undoing the resulting self-rejection in order to bring about self-acceptance, self-appreciation, and self-love.

In religious terms, this process can be described as one in which man rediscovers his cosubstantiality with the divine nature, and comes closer to seeing the world and himself as God did on the seventh day of Genesis, when He saw that His creation was good.

CLAUDIO NARANJO

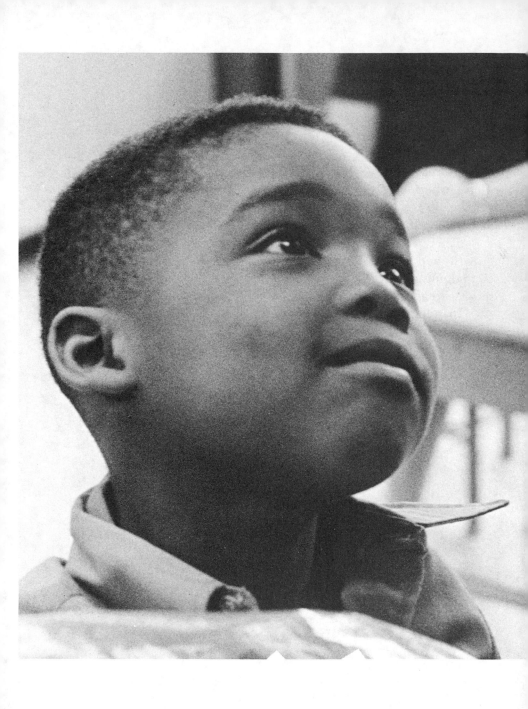

Every man has the right to feel that "because of me was the world created."

TALMUD

The basis of man's life with man is twofold, and it is one—the wish of every man to be confirmed as what he is, even as what he can become, by men; and the innate capacity in man to confirm his fellow-men in this way. . . . Genuine conversation . . . means acceptance of otherness. (Everything) depends, so far as human life is concerned, on whether each thinks of the other as the one he is (and) unreservedly accepts and confirms him in his being this man and in his being made in this particular way.

Man wishes to be confirmed in his being by man, and wishes to have a presence in the being of the other. . . . Secretly and bashfully he watches for a Yes which allows him to be and which can come to him only from one human person to another.

MARTIN BUBER

Prayer Flights

Once someone accepted me—
me, with my somewhat long nose
and skinny features.
Someone accepted
the way I speak,
the way I act in public, and
the way I really am.

Because I was accepted,
I can see more clearly who I am
and accept myself without reservation.
I no longer want to be another.

I am myself—simply and surely.
Love has finally defined for me
the man I really am, and always was.
And I am not troubled or ashamed
by this definition.

Please, God, never let me despair
because I am who I am.

MARK LINK, S.J.

I am not worthless
and I'm tired of feeling
that way
I'm tired of trying to prove that I can live up or down
to your expectations
I'm choosing to just Live,
My head feels like Disintegration
and my throat parches with pain
Seared by the Salt of all those unshed tears
but I know I'm Being Born, . . .

. . . maybe for the first time
Slowly the joy of beginning to know
Me as Beautiful,
. . . of loving Me
. . . and finding me Worthy
and then as healing happens
the chance of touching
of being seen free
as someone who can be
Loved.

BILL & CAROLE TEGELER

Be grateful for yourself. Yes for yourself. Be thankful. Understand that what a man is is something he can be grateful for, and ought to be grateful for.

WILLIAM SAROYAN

Please Hear What I Am Not Saying

Don't be fooled by me. Don't be fooled by the face I wear. I wear a mask. I wear a thousand masks—masks that I am afraid to take off; and none of them are me.

Pretending is an art that is second nature to me, but don't be fooled. For God's sake, don't be fooled. I give the impression that I am secure, that all is sunny and unruffled within me as well as without; that confidence is my name and coolness my game, that the water is calm and I am in command; and that I need no one. But don't believe me, please. My surface may seem smooth, but my surface is my mask, my ever varying and ever concealing mask.

Beneath lies no smugness, no complacence. Beneath dwells the real me in confusion, in fear, in aloneness. But I hide that. I don't want anybody to know it. I panic at the thought of my weakness and fear of being exposed. That's why I frantically create a mask to hide behind—a nonchalant, sophisticated façade —to help me pretend, to shield me from the glance that knows. But such a glance is precisely my salvation, my only salvation, and I know it. That is, if it's followed by acceptance, if it's followed by love.

It's the only thing that can liberate me from myself, from my own self-built prison wall, from the barriers I so painstakingly erect. It's the only thing that will assure me of what I can't assure myself—that I am really something.

But I don't tell you this. I don't dare. I'm afraid to. I'm afraid your glance will not be followed by acceptance and love. I'm afraid you'll think less of me, that you'll laugh, and your laugh would kill me; I'm afraid that deep down I'm nothing, that I'm just no good and that you will see this and reject me.

So I play my game, my desperate, pretending game, with a façade of assurance without, and a trembling child within.

And so begins the parade of masks, the glittering but empty parade of masks. My life becomes a front. I idly chatter to you in suave tones of surface talk. I tell you everything that is nothing and nothing that is everything, of what's crying inside me. So when I'm going through my routine, do not be fooled by what I am saying.

Please listen carefully and try to hear what I am not saying, what I would like to be able to say, what for survival I need to say, but I can't say.

I dislike hiding, honestly. I dislike the superficial game I am playing, the superficial phony I am being. I'd like to be really genuine and spontaneous and me. But you've got to help me. You've got to hold out your hand even when that's the last thing I seem to want or need. Only you can wipe away from my eyes the blank stare of the breathing dead. Only you can call me into aliveness. Each time you're kind and gentle and encouraging, each time you try to understand because you really care, my heart begins to grow wings, very small wings, very feeble wings —but wings.

With your sensitivity and compassion and your power of understanding, you can breathe life into me. I want you to know that. I want you to know how important you are to me. How you can be the creator of the person that is me, if you choose to. *Please choose.* You can remove the mask, you alone can release me from my lonely prison. So do not pass me by. Please do not pass me by. It will not be easy for you. My long conviction of worthlessness builds strong walls. The nearer you approach the blinder I might strike back. It's irrational, but despite what books say about a person, I am irrational. I fight against the very thing I cry out for.

But I am told that love is stronger than the strongest walls, and in this lies hope. MY ONLY HOPE. Please try to beat down my wall with firm but gentle hands—for a child is very sensitive, very fearful.

Who am I, you may wonder. I am someone you know very well. FOR I AM EVERY MAN YOU MEET. I AM EVERY WOMAN YOU MEET. I AM RIGHT IN FRONT OF YOU.

ANONYMOUS

"Thou shalt love thy neighbor as thyself" (Leviticus 19:18)

What does it mean to love our neighbor as we love ourselves? The Baal Shem explained:

How does one love himself? A person does not look for reasons to love himself. Man does not say: "I am nice, I am smart, I am generous, therefore I am deserving of my love." No. We love ourselves knowing our weaknesses, our shortcomings, our meanness, our vices. In the same manner we are to love our fellow men. To love for a reason is to love the reason, not the person. The reason departs, the love with it. True love is love without a reason. ∎

> May you find the path
> Which will lead you
> To the Highest and
> Truest of Yourself!
> Keep the right path
> Upwards – and hope
> For Perpetual Discovery –
> And Trust Life.
> That's All.

TEILHARD DE CHARDIN

To be deeply in love is, of course, a great liberating force and the most common experience that frees…Ideally, both members of a couple in love free each other to new and different worlds. I was no exception to the general rule. The sheer fact of finding myself loved was unbelievable and changed my world, feelings about life and myself. I was given confidence, strength, and almost a new character. The man I was to marry believed in me and what I could do, and consequently I found I could do more than I realized.

ANNE MORROW LINDBERGH

The trouble with you, my friend, is that you sweat too much blood for the whole world. Sweat some for yourself *first*. You cannot bring the Kingdom of God into the universe unless you first bring it into your heart.

LEO TOLSTOY

You are amazing grace
You are a precious jewel
You – special miraculous
 unrepeatable, fragile, fearful, tender, lost
Sparkling ruby emerald
Jewel rainbow splendor
Person

TRADITIONAL SPIRITUAL

4

Respect Yourself

This is the true joy in life, the being used for a purpose recognized by yourself as a mighty one; the being thoroughly worn out before you are thrown on the scrap heap; the being a force of nature instead of a feverish selfish little clod of ailments and grievances complaining that the world will not devote itself to making you happy.

GEORGE BERNARD SHAW

My Declaration of Self-Esteem

I am me.

In all the world, there is no one else exactly like me. There are persons who have some parts like me, but no one adds up exactly like me. Therefore, everything that comes out of me is authentically mine because I alone chose it.

I own everything about me—my body, including everything it does; my mind, including all its thoughts and ideas; my eyes, including the images of all they behold; my feelings, whatever they may be—anger, joy, frustration, love, disappointment, excitement; my mouth, and all the words that come out of it, polite, sweet or rough, correct or incorrect; my voice, loud or soft; and all my actions, whether they be to others or to myself.

I own my fantasies, my dreams, my hopes, my fears.

I own all my triumphs and successes, all my failures and mistakes.

Because I own all of me, I can become intimately acquainted with me. By so doing I can love me and be friendly with me in all my parts. I can then make it possible for all of me to work in my best interests.

I know there are aspects about myself that puzzle me, and other aspects that I do not know. But as long as I am friendly and loving to myself, I can courageously and hopefully look for the solutions to the puzzles and for ways to find out more about me.

However I look and sound, whatever I say and do, and whatever I think and feel at a given moment in time is me. This is authentic and represents where I am at that moment in time.

When I review later how I looked and sounded, what I said and did, and how I thought and felt, some parts may turn out to be unfitting. I can discard that which is unfitting, and keep that which proved fitting, and invent something new for that which I discarded.

I can see, hear, feel, think, say, and do. I have the tools to survive, to be close to others, to be productive, and to make sense and order out of the world of people and things outside of me.

I own me, and therefore I can engineer me.

I am me and I am okay.

VIRGINIA SATIR

Self-Esteem

Oh, let the self exalt itself,
Not sink itself below;
Self is the only friend of self,
And self self's only foe.

For self, when it subdues itself
befriends itself. And so
When it eludes self-conquest, is
Its own and only foe.

So calm, so self-subdued, the self
Has an unshaken base
Through pain and pleasure, cold and heat
Through honor and disgrace.

HINDU SCRIPTURES, FIRST CENTURY B.C.

An old weaver in Edinburgh prayed each Sunday: "Lord, grant me a high opinion of myself."

So much is a man worth as he esteems himself.

FRANCOIS RABELAIS

The greatest evil that can befall man is that he should come to think ill of himself.

GOETHE

Alas, I know if I ever became truly humble, I would be proud of it.

BENJAMIN FRANKLIN

5

Love Yourself

The doctrine that selfishness is the arch-evil and that to love oneself excludes loving others is by no means restricted to theology and philosophy, but it became one of the stock ideas promulgated in home, school, motion pictures, books; indeed in all instruments of social suggestion as well. "Don't be selfish" is a sentence which has been impressed upon millions of children, generation after generation. Its meaning is somewhat vague. Most people would say that it means not to be egotistical, inconsiderate, without any concern for others. Actually, it generally means more than that. Not to be selfish implies not to do what one wishes, to give up one's own wishes for the sake of those in authority. . . . "Don't be selfish" becomes one of the most powerful ideological tools in suppressing spontaneity and the free development of personality. Under the pressure of this slogan one is asked for every sacrifice and for complete submission: only those acts are "unselfish" which do not serve the individual but somebody or something outside himself.

. . . Love of others and love of ourselves are not alternatives. On the contrary, an attitude of love toward themselves will be found in all those who are capable of loving others. . . .

. . . If an individual is able to love productively, he loves himself too; if he can love only others, he can not love at all. . . .

. . . Selfishness and self-love, far from being identical, are actually opposites. The selfish person does not love himself too much but too little; in fact he hates himself. . . .

ERICH FROMM

Self love, my liege, is not so vile a sin as self neglecting.

WILLIAM SHAKESPEARE

He (Reinhold Niebuhr) is quite clear that the "original sin" is self-love, pretension, claiming too much, grasping after self-realization. I read such words and try to imagine the experience out of which they have grown. I have dealt with maladjusted and troubled individuals, in the intimate personal relationship of psychotherapy, for more than a quarter of a century. This has not been perhaps a group fully representative of the whole community, but neither has it been unrepresentative. And, if I were to search for the central core of difficulty in people as I have come to know them, it is that in the great majority of cases they despise themselves, regard themselves as worthless and unlovable. To be sure, in some instances this is covered by pretension, and in nearly all of us these feelings are covered by some kind of a facade. But I could not differ more deeply from the notion that self-love is the fundamental and pervasive "sin." Actually it is only in the experience of a relationship in which he is loved (something very close, I believe, to the theologians' *agape*) that the individual can begin to feel a dawning respect for, acceptance of, and finally, even a fondness for himself. It is as he can thus begin to sense himself as lovable and worthwhile, in spite of his mistakes, that he can begin to feel love and tenderness for others. It is thus that he can begin to realize himself and to reorganize himself and his behavior to move in the direction of becoming the more socialized self he would like to be. I believe that only if one views individuals on the most superficial or external basis are they seen as being primarily the victims of self-love. When seen from the inside, that is far from being their disease. At least so it seems to me.

CARL ROGERS

Any view of man which regards pride, selfishness, self-love, or self-idolatry as the major cause of man's problems misses the crucial fact that these are often symptoms of deeper causes—anxiety, self-hatred, inner conflict, and blocked growth. Pride is a symptom-level defense against these unbearably painful feelings. It is a frantic defense against the agony of feelings of weakness, vulnerability, and despair. Ultimately pride is a regressive defense against existential anxiety. The person makes an idol of himself and his own powers because he cannot trust anything else. Lacking a trustful relationship with God and others, he has no defense against his fear of death and meaninglessness. He retreats to the primitive defense of narcissism which only increases his anxieties. For an adult, narcissism (a normal response for a very small child) is like a suit of medieval armor in a modern battle. As a defense, it cuts the person off from the only sources of genuine help—meaningful relationships with others and with God. Narcissistic pride arises from anxiety and self-rejection but it becomes a malignant symptom which produces greater anxiety and self-rejection. A vicious cycle is thus established.

HOWARD J. CLINEBELL, JR.

Fromm has pointed out, in an important essay, that love of self and love of some other person are not mutually exclusive, as was long believed. He states emphatically that one can love another only if one loves himself. The rationale behind this precept may be stated in these terms: To love oneself means that one is concerned with his growth and happiness and will behave in ways which implement these values. Self-loving, in a real sense, gives actual practice in loving; to the extent that others are similar to the self, then these ways of acting which constitute self-love will make another person happy if they are directed to that person. Self-love makes one attentive to one's own needs and probably increases one's sensitivity to the needs of others; if one has experienced needs and gratifications, one can visualize more vividly what the partner's needs and gratifications feel like.

It should also be pointed out that healthy self-love is an outgrowth of having been loved by parents and other significant persons; and we have shown that the experience of having been loved enlarges one's capacity for active love.

When a person ignores or hates himself, he is less able to love others. The self-hater cannot love others, because he usually claims total obedience from those for whom he has "sacrificed" so much. The mother described by Philip Roth in *Portnoy's Complaint* was such a martyr, who "loved" her son more than she did herself; she sacrificed her happiness on his (unasked) behalf. All she wanted in return was complete conformity with her wishes and demands, which is incompatible with genuine love. Mrs. Portnoy was a tyrant, whose love for her son nearly destroyed him.

Psychoanalysts regard excessive unselfishness as a neurotic trait, and personality hygienists such as Maslow and Fromm place a positive value on "healthy" selfishness. This is no more than a recognition on the basis of clinical experience that the person who is concerned for his own growth and happiness will have acted so as to promote it; in consequence he is a better person and better able to give.

SIDNEY M. JOURARD

46

6

Be Yourself

The courage to be is the ethical act in which a man affirms his own being in spite of elements of his existence which conflict with his essential self-affirmation.

PAUL TILLICH

Parent to child: What do you want to be?
Child: I want to be myself. All the other parts are taken.

ANONYMOUS

To thine own self be true.
And it must follow as the night the day,
thou canst not then be false to any man.

WILLIAM SHAKESPEARE

...when an acorn and a chestnut fall side by side, the one does not remain inert to make way for the other, but both obey their own laws, and spring up and grow and flourish as best they can, till one perhaps overshadowes and destroys the other. If a plant cannot live according to its nature, it dies; and so a man.

HENRY DAVID THOREAU

It is clear to me that in therapy . . . commitment to purpose and to meaning in life is one of the significant elements of change. It is only when the person decides, "I am someone; I am someone worth being; I am committed to being myself," that change becomes possible.

CARL R. ROGERS

The chassidic saint Rav Zussye of Tarnifal trembled before his death:

I am about to face the Holy one, blessed be He, and justify my sojourn on the world. If He will ask me: Zussye why were you not like Moses? I shall respond, because you did not grant me the powers you granted Moses. If He will ask me: Zussye, why were you not like Rabbi Akiba? I shall respond because you did not grant me the powers you granted Rabbi Akiba. But the Almighty will not ask me why I was not like Moses, or why I was not like Rabbi Akiba. The Almighty will ask me: Zussye, why were you not like Zussye, why did you not fulfill the potential which was Zussye, and it is for this question that I tremble.

Starvation is a cause of death to be pitied and fought but far more people die because of what they do eat than die of what they lack. The same is true of education. Ignorance may be more dramatic, but knowledge is just as dangerous.

By the time a child becomes a teen-ager and enters high school he is filled with myths, misconceptions, fears, and doubts which schooling and parents have forced upon him. . . . Some knowledge which a vast number of teens have learned and which desperately needs to be unlearned is: I am not important; my feelings cannot be trusted and should be controlled; I need permission to do things; adults usually know better; I am controlled by outside forces; I must hide my real self; learning is something others give to me; I must become what others want me to.

JEFFREY SCHRANK

To be nobody—but yourself—in a world that is doing its best, night and day, to make you everybody else—means to fight the hardest battle which any human being can fight, and never stop fighting.

E. E. CUMMINGS

A Hasidic Predecessor of the Gestalt Prayer

If I am I because I am I,
And You are You because You are You,
Then I am and You are.

But if I am I because You are You,
And You are You because I am I,

Then I am not and You are not.

RABBI MENDEL OF KOTZK (1787-1859)

It is the chiefest point of happiness that a man is willing to be what he is.

DESIDERIUS ERASMUS

7

Nourish Yourself

The more each person strives and is able to seek his profit, that is to say, to preserve his being, the more virtue does he possess; on the other hand, in so far as each person neglects his own profit he is impotent.

BARUCH SPINOZA

If two are traveling on a journey (far from civilization), and one has a pitcher of water, if both drink, they will (both) die, but if one only drinks, he can reach civilization. The Son of Patura taught: It is better that both should drink and die, rather than that one should behold his companion's death. Until R. Akiba came and taught: *"that thy brother may live with thee"*: thy life takes precedence over his life.

TALMUD

They made me guardian of the vineyards, but my own vineyard I did not guard.

SONG OF SONGS 1:6

Bill of Rights for Winners

1. You have the right to be you—the way you are, the way you want to be.
2. You have the right to grow, to change, to become, to strive, to reach for any goal, to be limited only by your degree of talent and amount of effort.
3. You have the right to privacy—in marriage, family, or any relationship or group—the right to keep a part of your life secret, no matter how trivial or important, merely because you want it to be that way. You have the right to be alone part of each day, each week, and each year to spend time with and on yourself.
4. You have the right to be loved and to love, to be accepted, cared for, and adored, and you have the right to fulfill that right.
5. You have the right to ask questions of anyone at any time in any matter that affects your life, so long as it is your business to do so; and to be listened to and taken seriously.
6. You have the right to self respect and to do everything you need to do to increase your self-esteem, so long as you hurt no one in doing so.

7. You have the right to be happy, to find something in the world that is meaningful and rewarding to you and that gives you a sense of completeness.
8. You have the right to be trusted and to trust and to be taken at your word. If you are wrong, you have the right to be given a chance to make good, if possible.
9. You have the right to be free as long as you act responsibly and are mindful of rights of others and of those obligations that you entered into freely.
10. You have the right to win, to succeed, to make plans, to see those plans fulfilled, to become the best you that you can possibly become.

D. S. VISCOTT

Caring for Myself

Just as I may be indifferent to myself, use myself as a thing, or be a stranger to myself, so I may care for myself by being responsive to my own needs to grow. I become my own guardian, so to speak, and take responsibility for my life. Caring for myself is a species of the genus "caring."

Almost all the characteristics of caring—devotion, trust, patience, humility, honesty, and the primacy of the process—apply in a straightforward way to caring for myself. However, the union with *the other* that goes with my awareness of it as existing in its own right has to be understood somewhat differently, because the other in this case is not separate from me. To care for myself, I must be able to experience myself as other (I must be able to see myself from the inside as I appear from the outside), and at the same time I must feel at one with myself rather than cut off and estranged from myself. Also, some of the ideas about caring become strained and artificial when applied literally to caring for myself. For instance, "In helping the other to grow, I grow as well" becomes "In helping myself to grow, I grow as well"; or "In caring for another, we help him to care for himself" becomes "In caring for myself, I help to care for myself."

Egocentricity is morbid preoccupation with self and opaqueness to the needs of others. But there is nothing egocentric about caring for myself. First, the self-idolatry and the preoccupation with whether or not others admire me that are characteristic of egocentricity have nothing to do with helping myself to grow. In fact, the egocentric person is not fundamentally interested in himself; he avoids looking honestly at himself because he is essentially indifferent to his own needs to actualize himself. The self-complacency that often accompanies egocentricity is the converse of responding to one's own needs to grow.

Second, caring for myself takes into account my need to care for something or someone outside of myself. I can only fulfill myself by serving someone or something apart from myself, and if I am unable to care for anyone or anything separate from me, I am unable to care for myself.

Only the man who understands and appreciates what it is to grow, who understands and tries to satisfy his own needs for growth, can properly understand and appreciate growth in another; for I relate to other people in the same general way in which I relate to myself. Although caring for another person assumes that I care for myself (if I am unable to care for myself, I am unable to care for another person), the connection between caring for some other *thing* and caring for myself does not seem to be so close. The writer or the artist, it would seem, may care for his work without necessarily being able to care for himself.

MILTON MAYEROFF

Nourishing and Toxic Living

1. Nourishing: Do I take the initiative in doing the best I can to get what I need?
   or
   Toxic: Do I wait and hope that somehow what I need will be brought to me by someone else?

2. Nourishing: Do I decide what's most important for me?
   or
   Toxic: Do I allow others to make decisions for me?

3. Nourishing: Do I give up my attempts to control the world and accept life as it is?
   or
   Toxic: Do I live my life dominated by fears of catastrophe for which I continuously attempt to prepare?

4. Nourishing: Am I willing to take reasonable risks and experiment with new behavior that might be more satisfying?
   or
   Toxic: Do I cling to obsolete behavior patterns which mainly offer the security of being familiar?

5. Nourishing: Do I focus on what I am doing in the here and now?
   or
   Toxic: Do I usually wander into fantasies of the future or mistakes about the past?

6. Nourishing: Do I pay attention to one experience at a time?
   or
   Toxic: Do I try to do two things at once and thereby split my attention into pieces?

7. Nourishing: Do I take for myself the central role of determining my life style?
   or
   Toxic: Do I give over this function to others?

8. Nourishing: Do I take responsibility for satisfying my own needs?

Toxic: Do I try to manipulate other people into doing it for me?

9. Nourishing: Do I function as best I can in the here and now of my life?

or

Toxic: Do I cling to the misfortunes and tragedies of my past (real or imagined) and use these as excuses to avoid taking responsibility for myself in the present?

10. Nourishing: Do I live my personal life as I see fit and take my chances that some people will reject me?

or

Toxic: Do I go through life explaining myself and needing everyone's approval?

11. Nourishing: Do I see life as exciting and stimulating?

or

Toxic: Do I experience myself struggling to stay alive in a jungle of hostile forces?

12. Nourishing: Do I see myself as continuing to grow to the last day of my life?

or

Toxic: Do I create an artificial cutoff (*e.g.*, "After thirty it's all downhill") and live as if my opportunities for new discoveries and newfound joys were over?

13. Nourishing: Do I accept my need for other people as part of my life style?

or

Toxic: Do I "let it all hang out" and if others don't like it, "Who needs them"?

14. Nourishing: Do I experience my conflicts and "problems" as essentially of my own making?

or

Toxic: Do I project these onto other people and blame them for my troubles?

15. Nourishing: Is my behavior primarily self-regulating and based on my discoveries of what fits me?

    or

    Toxic: Do I cling to attitudes instilled in me in my childhood which I am afraid to reject?

16. Nourishing: Do I accept myself as I am and decide how I wish to change if at all?

    or

    Toxic: Do I believe that I *must* become a different person in order to live a nourishing, gratifying life?

17. Nourishing: Am I willing to take the risks of reaching out for what I want?

    or

    Toxic: Am I so fearful of rejection that I would rather starve myself emotionally than risk being turned down?

18. Nourishing: Do I experience my feelings and emotions as valuable parts of myself?

    or

    Toxic: Do I see them as weaknesses to be controlled and suppressed?

19. Nourishing: Am I aware of the changing reality of myself and the world around me?

    or

    Toxic: Do I rigidly insist on my established attitudes and values as fixed and unchangeable?

20. Nourishing: Do I accept my mistakes as an inevitable part of learning?

    or

    Toxic: When I do something that displeases me do I attack myself with ridicule, disgust or self-punishment?

21. Nourishing: Do I focus on the gratifications and meaningfulness of day-to-day experiences as the essence of living a nourishing life?

Toxic: Do I toil without satisfaction, working toward the day when, hopefully, I will "be happy"?

22. Nourishing: Do I center my attention on appreciating what I enjoy in my experiencing of myself and my world?

or

Toxic: Do I focus on what's lacking or what I find frustrating?

23. Nourishing: Do I accept myself as I am and continue my growth primarily as something I want for myself?

or

Toxic: Do I stand condemned in my own eyes as inadequate and seek to "prove" myself by accomplishments or success?

24. Nourishing: Do I experience my selfishness as an expression of the law of self-preservation?

or

Toxic: Do I believe that "selfishness" is a dirty word?

25. Nourishing: Do I accept pain as a normal aspect of living and an inevitable aspect of my growth?

or

Toxic: Do I experience pain (anxiety, tension, fearfulness) as something "evil"?

26. Nourishing: Am I aware that pain is often a valuable message directing my attention toward some frustrated need which I am neglecting?

or

Toxic: Do I consider pain as something to be immediately minimized or eliminated in any way possible?

27. Nourishing: Is my behavior a reaction to my experiencing of present reality?

or

Toxic: Do I project my past experiences onto the present?

JERRY GREENWALD

Compare these two hypothetical instances. Person "A" is being shot by a firing squad because he divulged national secrets to an enemy power. Person "B" is being shot by the enemy because he refused to divulge the military secrets of his beloved native country. Is there any doubt that person "B" will die with his head high, and that person "A" will feel deep shame? Person "B" is at peace, dying with self-respect.

Or, take another example. Person "A" is lying in a hospital bed recuperating from gun-shot wounds he received in shielding the life of the President from a mad would-be assassin. In the next bed is someone shot by a policeman who prevented him from robbing a bank. Is there any doubt that person "A" will be able to endure his pain with greater self-acceptance and self-esteem than person "B" (unless the latter is psychopathic)?

In other words, whatever pain and anguish we face in life will be endured and accepted more easily and more philosophically depending on the image we have of ourselves in that instance. Suffering for a good cause is carried much more lightly because a person's self-esteem is not damaged; to the contrary, it is raised. All the burdens of life are less weighty when one is satisfied with himself, accepts himself, likes himself, and is proud of his being and his life. On the other hand, a sense of guilt, shame, and a negative self-image will bring unhappiness, misery, and unbearable anxiety to the person who has created for himself a self-picture of an evil human being.

DOV PERETZ ELKINS

PART **II**

YOU ARE BEAUTIFUL!

8

You Are Unique

Who can say more than this rich praise, that you alone
are you?

WILLIAM SHAKESPEARE

For this reason was man created alone, to teach that whoever destroys a single soul of Israel, Scripture imputes guilt to
him as though he had destroyed a complete world; and whoever
saves a single soul of Israel, Scripture ascribes merit to him as
though he had preserved a complete world. Furthermore, it was
for the sake of peace among men, that one might not say to
his fellows, "My father was greater than yours." Another reason:
lest heretics say that there are many ruling powers in Heaven.
Again, to proclaim the greatness of the Holy One, blessed be
He; for if a man strikes many coins from the one mould, they
all resemble one another; but the supreme King of Kings, the
Holy One, blessed be He, fashioned every man in the stamp of
the first man, and yet not one of them resembles his fellows.
Therefore every single person is obliged to say: "The world was
created for my sake."

TALMUD

Every person born into this world represents something new, something that never existed before, something original and unique. It is the duty of every person...to know and consider that he is unique in the world in his particular character and that there has never been anyone like him in the world, for if there had been someone like him, there would have been no need for him to be in the world. Every single man is a new thing in the world, and is called upon to fulfill his particularity in this world...Every man's foremost task is the actualization of his unique, unprecedented and never recurring potentialities, and not the repetition of something that another, and be it even the greatest, has already achieved.

MARTIN BUBER

Each of us possesses a Holy Spark, but not everyone exhibits it to the best advantage. It is like the diamond which cannot cast its luster if buried in the earth. But when disclosed in its appropriate setting there is light, as from a diamond, in each of us.

RABBI ISRAEL OF RIZIN

God's divine throne is filled with empty spaces of varying sizes, shapes, designs. Each space represents the soul of a person who has fulfilled his unique task in the world. Each soul is a different colored jewel. Only when all the spaces are filled and the crown complete will the Messiah come.

THE MAGGID OF MEZERITCH, HASIDIC MASTER

SNOWFLAKE

We are each of us a snowflake
No two of us the same
Reflections of the ever loving source from which we came
Unique in form and beauty, crystalized at birth
Little flecks of heaven born to melt into the earth.

We are each of us a snowflake
Of infinite design
Transitory dancers on the window panes of time
Unique in form and beauty, no two of us the same
Reflections of the everloving source from which we came

We are each of us a snowflake
A falling star in flight
A traveler through the universe, in search of our own light
Unique in form and beauty, of infinite design
Transitory dancers on the window panes of time.

BARBARA MEISLIN

One young man was asked by a solicitous questioner what he could do better than anyone else. It was the assumption of the person who asked the question that everyone has some attribute at which he excels. Thus the question was intended to help the young man discover this attribute in order to increase his self-esteem. But the answer that the questioner received was one that he was probably not prepared for. For the young man, who seemed very comfortable and self-assured, replied, "I can be *me* better than anyone else in the world."

This is the real answer to the question. Each one of us can be the unique individual self that we are, better than anyone else. And it is impossible to compare such individuals because it is like comparing apples and oranges. *We are all best at being different and unique.* If we can come to perceive ourselves this way, we cannot be disparaged. And the feelings that accompany that experience will largely disappear from our lives.

This is, of course, an ideal statement of what our aims might be. Although we may never reach the state in which we are completely invulnerable to derisive attacks, from a practical standpoint all we need do is to make progress in approaching this goal. A clear vision of a person's intrinsic worth makes him almost impervious to disparagement of any kind. Moreover, this vision dispenses with the necessity for an exaggerated PR image. Once a person perceives himself as worthwhile, he has no need to continue to present falsified versions of himself to himself and the world.

LOU BENSON

9

Self-Esteem and Behavic

Insecurity destroys the person's capacity to be objective. If he is secure, he is likely to consider his ideas as being subject to revision; but his concern with facts may disappear in a situation that involves his self-concept and makes him unsure of himself. Then all awareness of what he knows as distinguished from what he does not know becomes submerged in his insecure need to be right. He is moved by unconscious attitudes, fears, conditionings, prejudices, and values—all of which interfere with his capacity to think clearly. For the moment he has abandoned the scientific attitude. Many observers have noted that values and attitudes—important to the person's self-concept—tend to persist in the face of contradictory data or logic.

JOSEPH STEIN

They can conquer who believe they can.

JOHN DRYDEN

There are those who think they can, and those who think they can't. They are both right.

HENRY FORD

Perhaps the most important single cause of a person's success or failure...has to do with the question of what he believes about himself.

ARTHUR W. COMBS

Self-esteem is not a new term in psychology; it has appeared in the writings of Freud, Erikson, Fenichel, Sullivan, and others. It is only recently, however, that close examination of its micro-structure has suggested self-esteem as a suitably definitive concept by which to explain variances in the level of productive behavior. Although the nature of self-esteem requires further exploration, it appears from the findings thus far that self-esteem should properly be conceptualized as a basic, continuous psychological need of all persons. This concept applies not only to the normal processes of growth and development in the well-functioning child, but also to the modification of low-productive and non-productive behavior in the poorly functioning child, adolescent, or adult. It should provide the basis for a new theoretical model of personality functioning which will not only serve to explain growth and development of successful persons more adequately than have past models, but will also provide a firmer basis for the treatment and remediation of the problems of malfunctioning persons.

JOHN V. GILMORE

Whatever you can do, or dream you can do, begin it. Boldness has genius, power and magic in it. Begin it now.

GOETHE

The following principles summarize the basic approach and recognition of the self in true experience and the creation of human understandingness.

1. The individual knows himself better than anyone else.

2. Only the individual himself can develop his potentialities.

3. The individual's perception of his own feelings, attitudes, and ideas is more valid than any outside diagnosis can be.

4. Behavior can best be understood from the individual's own point of view.

5. The individual responds in such ways as to be consistent with himself.

6. The individual's perception of himself determines how he will behave.

7. Objects have no meaning in themselves. Individuals give meanings and reality to them. These meanings reflect the individual's background.

8. Every individual is logical in the context of his own personal experience. His point of view may seem illogical to others when he is not understood.

9. As long as the individual accepts himself, he will continue to grow and develop his potentialities. When he does not accept himself, much of his energies will be used to defend rather than explore and to actualize himself.

10. Every individual wants to grow toward self-fulfillment. These growth strivings are present at all times.

11. An individual learns significantly only those things which *are* involved in the maintenance or enhancement of *self*. No one can force the individual to permanent or creative learning. He will learn only if he wills to. Any other type of learning is temporary and inconsistent with the self and will disappear as soon as threat is removed.

12. Concepts, ideas, symbols, and events can be denied or distorted but experience is experienced in the unique reality of the individual person and cannot be untrue to itself. If it threatens the maintenance or enhancement of self, the experience will be of little relevance or consequence to the individual though it may temporarily stifle further growth.

13. We cannot teach another person directly and we cannot facilitate real learning in the sense of making it easier. We can make learning for another person possible by providing information, the setting, atmosphere, materials, resources, and *by being* there. The learning process itself is a unique individualistic experience. It may be a difficult experience for the individual person even if it has significance for the enhancement of self.

14. Under threat the self is less open to spontaneous expression; that is, is more passive and controlled. When free from threat the self is more open, that is, free to be and to strive for actualization.

CLARK E. MOUSTAKAS

Yes, I'm my own best friend. I've always been that way, even when I felt other people didn't understand me, because I knew I still had to be true to myself. There were times when I allowed people to get me off the track about who I was but I'd analyze myself and find out what was happening before I got myself into too much trouble.

I find that people who don't like themselves much are very difficult to be with. They are constantly searching to find out who they are, and therefore they are never very honest. They are intellectually floating personalities. Some people say that being a performer has something to do with being your own best friend, but I think for me it was mostly being without a family and having to find my own way through life in order to survive. It was the basic need for healthy survival that made me realize I had to be my own best friend.

EARTHA KITT

A student not only learns about things and ideas in school, but also learns about himself. Indeed, one of the striking things we are currently discovering is that the most important ideas which affect a student's behavior are those ideas or conceptions he has about himself, which, in part, are a consequence of his school experiences. Unfortunately thousands upon thousands of students graduate from high school with the "I can't" rather than the "I can" feeling about themselves. During the 1960s for example, 7.5 million youngsters did not even finish high school—many because of the "I can't, so why try anyway?" attitude. . . .

A monumental research effort . . . involving over one thousand seventh-grade students focused specifically on self-concept and ability in school and academic achievement. They found a significant and positive relationship between self-concept and academic performance and, in addition, observed that self-concept was significantly and positively related to the perceived evaluations which significant others held of the student. This quite literally means that if persons "significant" (valued, prized, important) to a student think highly of him, then he is apt to think highly of himself.

DON E. HAMACHEK

Probably the most important requirement for effective behavior, central to the whole problem, is self-esteem.

STANLEY COOPERSMITH

10

Avoiding the Put-Down

Disparagement as a Weapon

Insults, embarrassments, humiliations, and depreciations are all used by people against one another. The aim of such treatment is usually to injure the other person by piercing the armor of his PR personality. Such conduct on the part of one person against another is an aggressive act that employs psychological weaponry. The most serious use of such a tactic occurs when it is directed against children.

The child is the crucible in which the concept of self-esteem is forged. And true self-esteem is . . . a confidence in one's own worth. A child's self-esteem develops out of contacts with significant others who communicate his worth to him in many ways. But a lack of this feeling can easily be engendered in a child by parents or others who continually make derisive remarks about him.

Imagine, on the one hand, a child who is continually praised and encouraged by his parents for his many and varied efforts; and on the other hand, a child who is always berated, made fun of, and told of his stupidity. The former is likely to develop a feeling of confidence in his own capacities, while the latter may come to perceive himself as incompetent, inept, and worthless.

The victim of these devaluing perceptions will often be subjected to what is sometimes called pathological anxiety. Brandon refers to it as "a crisis of self-esteem—any threat to a man's ego—anything which he experiences as a danger to his mind's efficacy and control—is a potential source of pathological anxiety." . . .

Although disparagement is a devastating weapon when used against a child, it is also quite potent when directed against adults as well. Many of the arguments that people engage in are really exchanges of verbal barbs directed from one person to another in an attempt to undermine the other's self-image. Some cocktail parties are virtual battlegrounds for insult flinging where women can criticize one another's clothing and men can ridicule each other's romantic prowess.

Once again, it is the person with doubts about himself who is more vulnerable to these kinds of attacks. Some people are literally terrified when entering a room full of people for fear that they will say or do something that will bring shame down on them and make them the butt of ridicule. To humiliate, shame, or embarrass someone is therefore a powerful kind of disparagement, especially in front of a large number of other people.

There are many ways in which these weapons are made potent. Almost any indication that a person is not up to par in some conventionally accepted virtue is enough to evoke strong feelings of inferiority. The man who is cowardly, the girl who is promiscuous, the woman whose house is messy, the man who is impotent or the woman who is frigid, the boy who strikes out, the girl who is unpopular, the businessman who is revealed as a swindler, the sick person; all may feel that they are something less than they would like to be. And others, by calling attention to their particular shortcoming, can cause them a great deal of anguish. . . .

Help itself can also be perceived as a disparagement if it is offered in a condescending way. If the attitude that accompanies it seems to say, "You poor thing, I've got to help you because you are so unfortunate" (that is, helpless, unheroic, and so on), the help will more often be resented than appreciated.

Of course anything that lowers the status of another person is seen as disparagement. Therefore, any kind of treatment, from discrediting a person's reputation to taking away his key to the executive washroom, qualifies.

LOU BENSON

Too many put-downs give you a bad case of lip-lash. It is better for everyone if you go for the jocular vein instead of the jugular vein.

JOEL GOODMAN

Rabbi Nechuniah ben Hakkaneh was asked: How have you merited long life? He replied: "I never tried to elevate myself at the expense of my neighbor."

TALMUD

Looking down on others is the lazy person's path to self-esteem.

GEORGE F. WILL

All who descend to Gehenna will arise except for one who shames his neighbor publicly, and one who calls his neighbor by a nickname.

TALMUD

The Enemy

He and I are old friends,
For I have known him many years.
We have met countless times
  on the field to do battle.
Never have I been able to
Repel his first assault, so great his strength.
He strikes with the lust that a man feels for a woman.
With viciousness that only a fire of passion can create.
It would appear my foe knows every weak point,
  and begins his attack there.
If in my lifetime I am ever able to defeat him,
  the victory would make me whole.
For this is the enemy that every mortal knows,
Few have truly defeated.
For my enemy lurks within a fortress
  I cannot breach.
He lives within me.

GOMELIA BAKER

I have made a ceaseless effort not to ridicule, not to bewail, nor to scorn human actions, but to understand them.

BARUCH SPINOZA

11

Responsible Selfishness

The dichotomy between selfishness and unselfishness disappears altogether in healthy people because in principle every act is *both* selfish and *unselfish.* Our subjects are simultaneously very spiritual and very pagan and sensual even to the point where sexuality becomes a *path* to the spiritual and "religious." Duty cannot be contrasted with pleasure nor work with play when duty *is* pleasure, when work *is* play, and the person doing his duty and being virtuous is simultaneously seeking his pleasure and being happy. If the most socially identified people are themselves also the most individualistic people, of what use is it to retain the polarity? If the most mature are also childlike? And if the most ethical and moral people are also the lustiest and most animal?

ABRAHAM H. MASLOW

Haughtiness means to contrast oneself with others. The haughty man is not he who knows himself, but he who compares himself with others. No man can presume too much if he stands on his own ground since all the heavens are open to him and all the worlds devoted to him. The man who presumes too much is the man who contrasts himself with others, who sees himself as higher than the humblest of things, who rules with measure and weights and pronounces judgment.

"If Messiah should come today," a zaddik said, "and say, 'You are better than the others,' then I would say to him, 'You are not Messiah.'"

MARTIN BUBER

Who, if I may be so inconsiderate as to ask, isn't egocentric? Half a century of time and several continents of space, in addition to a healthily developed curiosity, haven't yet enabled me to locate a single peripherally situated ego. Perhaps I somehow simply didn't meet the right people, and vice versa. At any rate, my slight acquaintance with senators, pickpockets, and scientists leads me to conclude that they are far from unselfcentered. So, I believe, are all honest educators. And so (I'm convinced) are streetcleaners, deafmutes, murderers, mothers, mountain-climbers, cannibals, fairies, strong men, beautiful women, unborn babes, international spies, ghostwriters, bums, business executives, out and out nuts, cranks, dopefiends, policemen, altruists (above all), ambulance-chasers, obstetricians and liontamers. Not forgetting morticians—as undertakers (in this epoch of universal culture) prefer to denominate themselves. Or, as my friend the distinguished biographer M. R. Werner once subrosafully remarked, over several biscuit dubouches "when you come right down to it, everybody's the whole boxoftricks to himself; whether she believes it or not." . . .

E. E. CUMMINGS

Selfishness

I heard a woman on the beach
　　say to her little girl
Don't be selfish
What sad advice

I would give her better
Be selfish, little girl
Love yourself well
Love yourself first
Then will you love others
　　far, far better

Not with grudging show
Nor with unfeeling ritual
Or numb duty, or self-congratulating
　　sacrifice
Or stuttering terror of loss

Be selfish, little girl
Be best to yourself
And rest assured that you
　　will always be
Joyfully, unstintingly
And if you will give to others
Give them most
Help to be best
　　to themselves too.

STANLEY M. HERMAN

I think there's a difference between being *selfish* and being *self-centered*. To me selfish is a very good quality because if you don't love you, you sure as hell can't love anybody else. Being self-centered is a whole different trip. But no, I am all for selfishness. Doing what's good for you is good for everybody.

LYNN CAINE

Many age-old philosophical problems must be seen in a new light. Some of them perhaps may even be seen to be pseudo problems resting on misconceptions about human motivational life. Here may be included, for instance, the sharp distinction between selfishness and unselfishness. If our instinctoid impulses, for instance, to love, arrange it so that we get more personal 'self-ish' pleasure from watching our children eat a goody than from eating it ourselves, then how shall we define 'selfish' and how differentiate it from 'unselfish'? Is the man who risks his life for the truth any less selfish than the man who risks his life for food, if the need for truth is as animal as the need for food?

ABRAHAM H. MASLOW

12

Your Self-Image

The importance of one's self-image is aptly illustrated in the fairy tale of *Rapunzel*. It is the story of a young girl, imprisoned in a tower with an old witch. The young girl is in fact very beautiful, but the old witch insistently tells her that she is ugly. It is, of course, a stratagem of the witch to keep the girl in the tower with herself. The moment of Rapunzel's liberation occurs one day when she is gazing from the window of the tower. At the base of the tower stands her Prince Charming. She throws her hair, long and beautiful golden tresses, out the window (the root-ends, of course, remain attached to her head), and he braids the hair into a ladder and climbs up to rescue her. Rapunzel's imprisonment is really not that of the tower but the fear of her own ugliness which the witch has described so often and so effectively. However, when Rapunzel sees in the mirroring eyes of her lover that she is beautiful, she is freed from the real tyranny of her own imagined ugliness.

This is true not only in the case of Rapunzel but with all of us. We desperately need to see in the mirror of another's eyes our own goodness and beauty, if we are to be truly free. Until this moment, we, too, will remain locked inside the prison towers of ourselves. And, if the thrust of love requires us to be outside of ourselves and to be preoccupied with the happiness and fulfillment of others, we will not love very much until we have had this vision.

JOHN POWELL

An Allegory

. . . a mouse ran into the office of the Educational Testing Service and accidentally triggered a delicate point in the apparatus just as the College Entrance Examination Board's data on one Henry Carson was being scored.

Henry was an average high-school student who was unsure of himself and his abilities. Had it not been for the mouse, Henry's scores would have been average or less, but the mouse changed all that, for the scores which emerged from the computer were amazing—800's in both the verbal and quantitative areas.

When the scores reached Henry's school, the word of his giftedness spread like wildfire. Teachers began to reevaluate their gross underestimation of this fine lad, counselors trembled at the thought of neglecting such talent, and even college admissions officers began to recruit Henry for their schools.

New worlds opened for Henry, and as they opened he started to grow as a person and as a student. Once he became aware of his potentialities and began to be treated differently by the significant people in his life, a form of self-fulfilling prophecy took place. Henry gained in confidence and began "to put his mind in the way of great things." . . . Henry became one of the best men of his generation.

WILLIAM W. PURKEY

Signs of a Healthy, Positive Self-Image

Increasing literature and research devoted to the problem of self-concept leaves little doubt but that mental health depends deeply on the quality of a person's feelings about himself. Just as an individual must maintain a healthy view of the world around him, so must he learn to perceive himself in positive ways. A person who has a strong, self-accepting attitude presents a behavioral picture very much the opposite of one who feels inadequate and inferior. Although there are certainly variations from one individual to another and for the same individual between situations, generally speaking, a person who has a healthy self-image can be characterized in the following ways:

1. He has certain values and principles he believes in strongly and is willing to defend them even in the face of strong group opinion; however, he feels personally secure enough to modify them if new experience and evidence suggest he is in error. (An insecure person finds it difficult to change his position for fear that it may be interpreted as weakness, or lack of ability, or competency. "You may be right, but I'm not wrong.")

2. He is capable of acting on his own best judgment without feeling excessively guilty or regretting his actions if others disapprove of what he's done. When he does feel guilty, he is not overwhelmed by the guilt. He can say, "I made a mistake—I'll have to improve," rather than "I made a mistake—how terrible I am."

3. He does not spend undue time worrying about what is coming tomorrow, or being upset by today's experience, or fussing over yesterday's mistakes. I remember a little poem which used to hang on the wall in my grandparents' living room. It goes like this:

It's easy enough to be pleasant
When Life flows along like a song,
But the man worth while
Is the man who can smile
When everything goes dead wrong.

4. He retains confidence in his ability to deal with problems, even in the face of failures and setbacks. He does not conclude, "Because I failed I am a failure," but is more likely to say, "I failed. I'll have to work harder."

5. He feels equal to others *as a person*—not superior or inferior—irrespective of the differences in specific abilities, family backgrounds, or attitudes of others toward him. He is able to say, "You are more skilled than I, but I am as much a person as you," which is different from thinking, "You are more skilled than I, therefore you are a better person." He is able to see that another individual's skills or abilities neither devalues nor elevates his own status as a person.

6. He is able to take it more or less for granted that he is a person of interest and value to others—at least to those with whom he chooses to associate. Another way of saying this is that he is not paralyzed by self-consciousness when in the company of other people.

7. He can accept praise without the pretense of false modesty ("Well, gosh, *anyone* could have done it."), and compliments without feeling guilty ("Thanks, but I *really* don't deserve it.")

8. He is inclined to resist the efforts of others to dominate him, especially those who are his peers. The resistance, in effect, is a way of saying, "I am as good as you—therefore there is no reason why I should be dominated by you."

9. He is able to accept the idea (and admit to others) that he is capable of feeling a wide range of impulses and desires, ranging all the way from being very angry to being very loving, from being very sad to being very happy, from feeling deep resentment to feeling great acceptance. It does not follow, however, that he *acts* on all his feelings and desires.

10. He is able to genuinely enjoy himself in a wide variety of activities involving work, play, creative self-expression, companionship, or, of all things, just plain loafing. An unknown author—a very wise man, no doubt—has expressed this idea in the following manner:

A master in the art of living draws no sharp distinction between his work and his play, his labour and his leisure, his mind and his body, his education and his recreation. He hardly knows which is which. He simply pursues his vision of excellence through whatever he is doing and leaves others to determine whether he is working or playing. To himself he always seems to be doing both.

11. He is sensitive to the needs of others, to accepted social customs and particularly to the idea that he cannot, willy-nilly, go about "self-actualizing" himself at the expense of everyone around him.

Perhaps we would do well to keep in mind that these are not destinations that only a fortunate few have passage to, or end states arrived at by a select number, but, rather, possibilities which any person desiring to better himself can hold as goals within his reach. Usually, motivation is more effective, and happiness more attainable, if a person concentrates on improvement rather than perfection.

DON E. HAMACHEK

Money and the Self-Image

Our perceptions of ourselves depend upon a great many things. We are greatly influenced during the developmental years by the attitudes of those close to us. Attitudes toward money are often extremely influential in the way we come to view human beings. If our parents and the rest of society tend to evaluate people by their wealth, we may use such a measure to appraise our own value. The manner in which we present ourselves to the world will therefore be affected by such considerations. If we have money, we will expect (and probably receive) a certain amount of respect and subsurvience from others. If we do not, we may expect very different kinds of treatment.

Money, therefore, and the things that it can buy help to create the image that we present to the world. In order to present a very favorable image, the accumulation of a great deal of money may become our most pressing motive. Money in this sense does not necessarily mean actual cash. It refers to wealth and *possession*. The important thing is to have the things that money can buy, especially those things that can be seen by others. An image gets its value by its effect on others. If others are impressed by our possessions, we are, too.

In some cases money becomes an expanded portion of the self (Knight, 1968). The person literally comes to identify himself with his goods. Sometimes the money refers to parts of the body, like limbs, that could be lost. And if the money has come to be extremely important in the identification, the man and his fortune become one. Certain people are referred to as "the millionaire, Mr. So-and-So," as if the word "millionaire" were part of his name. Such an identification of the man with what he owns is precarious, for there is always the danger that one may lose his fortune, and this can be tantamount to losing himself. It is perhaps not an accident that many of the people who lost their fortunes as a result of the Depression considered suicide the only thing left to them.

Some psychoanalysts believe that the fear of bodily injury as symbolized by the loss of money may refer to the "castration anxiety" described by Freud. Fear of genital injury (castration) was believed by Freud to arise because of the repression of forbidden sexual fantasies in childhood. Such a fear, it is believed, might be expressed symbolically in later life by the loss of one's *most cherished possession*, his money. Although the castration complex was related in Freud's thinking to Oedipal striving, it need not always be. If a person harbors fears of genital injury for whatever reason, he may in adult life come to symbolize these feelings in terms of money. Loss of his fortune would then be a serious threat to his self-image.

LOU BENSON

Watch Out for Self-Pity

You certainly do not rebuild self-love by indulging in self-pity. Self-pity does not generate self-respect. Self-pity focuses on the unhappy past, keeping alive the very experiences which must be forgotten and left behind. Self-pity focuses on what has happened. While you are concentrating on the unfortunate past, you are in that moment enslaved, controlled and dominated by that self-demoralizing past. When you recall the past, you are at that moment recaptured by it. It may have happened, but don't allow yourself to remain trapped in that experience by self-pity.

"Forgetting these things that are behind—I press toward the mark," Paul wrote. If unpleasant things come to pass—by all means let them do so. Why are we so inclined to self-pity? Are we trying to tenderly nurse a wounded self-love? If so, we must see that self-pity only keeps the wounded pride raw and open. In our own self-pity we hope to gain the pity of others, mistaking sympathy for respect. We crave to reassure the faltering self that it is worthy after all. If we feel this way, we must understand that pity is not necessarily respect. Sympathy is not necessarily esteem. Or do we indulge in self-pity—trapping ourselves in the past—for fear of moving ahead into a future where we might suffer additional assaults? Is self-pity a deceptive defense mechanism willfully experienced to protect me from the new risks I may encounter if I start thinking of beginning again?

ROBERT H. SCHULLER

13

Loving Your Body

There is a considerable amount of evidence to suggest that one's *appearance* is an important determiner of self-esteem, both among men and women. For example, in a study by Secord and Jourard, it was found that the feelings an individual had about his body were commensurate with the feelings that he had about himself as a person. That is, the person who had negative feelings about his body was also likely to feel negatively about himself as a total person and vice versa. In a series of studies by the same investigators, college students were asked to indicate the dimensions of different parts of their bodies, and to rate their feelings of satisfaction with these dimensions. In general, those who were satisfied with their bodies were also apt to be fairly secure and self-confident. In other words, persons who accepted their bodies were more likely to maintain higher self-esteem than persons who disliked their bodies. . . .

Physical appearance is important to one's development of self-esteem because it plays a part in determining the nature of the responses a person receives from other people. However, we should keep in mind that it is only *one* of *many* determiners of self-esteem. A healthy, balanced person will build his feelings of self-regard on a variety of grounds, among which would include achievement, creativeness, social status, moral and ethical behavior, interpersonal relationships, and the like. While a certain degree of concern about one's total body-image is compatible with developing a healthy personality, too much concern may be a signal that the individual's self-esteem is standing on *too limited a foundation*. For example, the woman whose entire self is wrapped up in being beautiful or sexy is left with very little once the beauty and sex appeal are gone. The body-builder whose entire self rests on having large biceps and photographic muscle differentiation runs the risk of emotional bankruptcy when he gets older and discovers that there is more to life than bulging muscles and high protein diets. Body image and appearance are only one part of a person's total feelings about himself. . . .

DON E. HAMACHEK

What exactly does the neurotic despise in himself? Sometimes everything: his human limitations; his body, its appearance and functioning. . . .

With regard to looks and appearance, we find the whole range from a person's feeling unattractive to feeling repulsive. At first glance it is astonishing to find this tendency in women who are attractive beyond average. But we must not forget that what counts are not objective facts or opinions of others but the discrepancy a woman feels between her idealized image and her actual self. Thus, even though by common acclaim she may be a beauty, she still is not the *absolute* beauty—such as never was and never will be. And so she may focus on her imperfections —a scar, a wrist not slender enough, or hair not naturally wavy— and run herself down on this score, sometimes to the extent of hating to look at a mirror. Or the fear of being repulsive to others may be aroused easily, for instance by the mere fact of having somebody who has been sitting beside her in the movies change his seat.

The self-berating on the score of looks becomes more poignant when one realizes that it is also fed from a deeper source. The question "Am I attractive?" is inseparable from another one: "Am I lovable?" Here we touch upon a crucial problem in human psychology. . . .

KAREN HORNEY

With some qualifications I suggest that nothing is more characteristic of mental well-being than a healthy self-respect, a regard for one's body and its functions, and a reasonably optimistic outlook on life.

BRUNO BETTELHEIM

One of my most beautiful friends is hardly what our society would call a classic beauty. At 5 feet, 4 inches tall and 120 to 125 pounds, she is absolutely average, statistically speaking. Clearly, she is not centerfold material: her belly protrudes a bit, her waist and neck are somewhat foreshortened, her thighs are slightly flabby and her face is round but lacks the delicacy of a cherub.

Yet nearly all who know her see her as beautiful. Why? Because she sees herself as an attractive woman who looks good for her 40 years. She is pleased with her physical persona and it shows in how she walks, talks, dresses, laughs and listens. Her dazzling smile projects beauty from the inside out.

Millions of Americans, especially the majority of women who view their physical being with disdain, even disgust, could learn from my friend and from the psychologists who try to help people end self-loathing and acquire a healthy body image.

JANE E. BRODY

14

Relating to Others

Acceptance of Self and Others

Another important area in which self-actualizing people differ from others is in their nonjudgmental acceptance of themselves. Maslow says that they seem to have a lack of overriding guilt and crippling shame and also to be free of the anxieties that usually accompany these feelings.

They can accept their own human nature in the stoic style, with all its shortcomings, with all its discrepancies from the ideal image without feeling real concern. . . .

Such feelings of comfort and acceptance with the self are extremely important in terms of laying down a tone that underlies a person's whole existence. The difference between happiness and unhappiness is related to this tone.

The healthy individual does not strive to live up to an ideal, perfect PR image. He sees himself as human and therefore as unheroic in the naive sense. He acknowledges his "shortcomings," his "deficiencies," his "inconsistencies." In short, he acknowledges his imperfections without being disparaged by them. Being accepting of his frailties, he can also be accepting of those of others. And the healthy person demands neither more nor less of others —he is willing to acknowledge human nature in all human beings, both in others and in himself.

One very important area in which self-actualizing people are accepting is on the animal level. They accept their animal nature without shame, without guilt, with a kind of gusto or *joie de vivre*. They are lusty in their love of food, sex, excitement. They tend not to feel shame or disgust with the functions of the body on an animal level. Thus they are less likely to respond negatively to these basic organismic needs.

LOU BENSON

By trusting your own heart, you shall gain more confidence in other men.

RALPH WALDO EMERSON

The person cannot love another beyond the love he has of himself. Whereas orthodox religion has traditionally taught 'Love your neighbor as yourself,' modern humanistic psychology proposes 'Love yourself to be better able to love your neighbor.' The person who self-actualizes will invariably like himself better and, in turn, become capable of liking others better. *Loving is a capacity,* not merely a state of feeling. The person who is emotionally secure, has a sense of belonging, and is adequate will display the capacity to love.

JOSEPH STEIN

A man's interest in the world is only the overflow of his interest in himself.

GEORGE BERNARD SHAW

Whoever hates himself will ultimately hate others even moreso.

THE BAAL SHEM TOV, HASIDIC MASTER

As you love yourself, so shall you love others. Strange, but true, but with no exceptions.

HARRY STACK SULLIVAN

A story is told of a prominent social worker who received a letter from a society woman who wanted to join in his crusade to help the poor children of New York. The society woman spoke at some length of her imperfections and ended by saying that perhaps her zeal for *his* cause would make up for her shortcomings. He wrote a brief reply:

Dear Madam,
Your truly magnificent shortcomings at present are too great. Nothing could prevent you from visiting them on victims of your humility. I advise that you love yourself more before you squander any love on others.

JOSHUA LOTH LIEBMAN

When a person makes peace with himself, he will be able to make peace with the whole world.

RABBI SIMCHA BUNAM

Nothing is a greater impediment to being on good terms with others than being ill at ease with yourself.

HONORÉ DE BALZAC

15

Your Children's Self-Image

My dream is to make families a place where adults with high self-esteem can develop. I think we have reached a point where if we don't get busy on dreams of this sort, our end is in sight. We need a world that is as good for human beings as it is for technology.

VIRGINIA SATIR

In earlier China, mothers would tightly bind their young daughters' feet and keep them bound for years, causing terrible deformity. It was done with good intent, because tiny feet and a mincing walk were considered attractive in a Chinese girl. In time, the crippled daughter would grow up, marry, and have daughters of her own. Then the irony: the crippled mother would get out the bandages and cripple her daughters just as she was crippled. Through generation after generation, like echoes in a canyon, the crippling continued. An old Russian proverb states the problem succinctly: "The little girl who is beaten will beat her doll-baby." We do unto others as we have been done unto.

So it happens that many small children are crippled by parents who were themselves crippled psychologically as children.

As a general rule, we can say that any behavior of significant people that causes a young child to think ill of himself, to feel inadequate, incapable, unworthy, unwanted, unloved, or unable, is crippling to the self. Where respect and warmth are missing, where the child's questions go unanswered, where his offers to help are rejected, where his discipline is based on failure and punishment, where he is excluded from his parents' emotional life, and where his basic rights are abused, there his self is undermined. It is vital for parents to remember the simple rule that they must have respect for and confidence in their children before their children can have self-respect or self-confidence.

WILLIAM W. PURKEY

A child's life is like a piece of paper on which every passerby leaves a mark.

ANCIENT CHINESE PROVERB

High Self-Esteem

1. High self-esteem is clearly a consistent characteristic of a productive person in any field of endeavor. Moreover, it appears to underlie, and to be prerequisite to, the development of all the other attributes of a productive individual: his sense of identity; his social competence, concern and maturity; and his numerous coping skills and characteristics.

2. High self-esteem develops in a family environment characterized by empathy, concern, and reinforcement. It appears to be the result of a continuous nurturance during the child's formative years in a loving and supportive, but also structured and consistent, social environment characterized by firmly upheld standards, values, and parental expectations. There is evidence that this environment is operative almost from infancy, and that it is the child's parents (or those who relate to him as parents) who are primarily responsible for his emotional development, as well as his physical and intellectual development, through the process of identification and socialization.

3. In the light of present evidence, there is every reason to believe that the characteristics which underlie productivity can be acquired by any child in any environment, given the basic conditions for the development of self-esteem.

JOHN V. GILMORE

The most deadly of all sins is the mutilation of a child's spirit.

ERIK ERIKSON

Children Learn What They Live

If a child lives with criticism,
   he learns to condemn.
If a child lives with hostility,
   he learns to fight.
If a child lives with ridicule,
   he learns to be shy.
If a child lives with shame,
   he learns to feel guilty.
If a child lives with tolerance,
   he learns to be patient.
If a child lives with encouragement,
   he learns confidence.
If a child lives with praise,
   he learns to appreciate.
If a child lives with fairness,
   he learns justice.
If a child lives with security,
   he learns to have faith.
If a child lives with approval,
   he learns to like himself.
If a child lives with acceptance and friendship,
   he learns to find love in the world.

DOROTHY LAW NOLTE

Counselor:	How does your mom feel about your school work?
Girl:	It could be better, I guess, I don't know exactly—we don't discuss it much.
Counselor:	Do your parents say anything to you about your report card?
Girl:	Sometimes they do.
Counselor:	I noticed you did about C work last year.
Girl:	Yeah, mostly I do that and sometimes not that good. I used to do better.
Counselor:	Could you tell me more about that?
Girl:	Well, last year I got a B in social studies and that's pretty good. Math got me though. I guess if I really tried—but I don't think I can because I've tried all I can. I'm telling you, it really gets me. My mother wasn't good in math either, but she's better in it now.
Counselor:	How do you know your mother used to be poor in it?
Girl:	She told me. *She says it's no wonder I'm not very good at it.*
Counselor:	What does she mean by that?
Girl:	Well, she says, well, I'm dumb—*"I guess I've handed it to you"* or something like that. I mean I'm real slow in math—it takes hours to get something in my head. One time my father and I were working on a problem and he lost his patience. He said I was so stupid that I should be in a special school. He was really mad.
Counselor:	How did that make you feel?
Girl:	Well, it hurt me. I was a little bit mad, but I got over it. *Maybe I am stupid. . . .*

DON E. HAMACHEK

The parent can make himself more aware of the child's self concept by answering, perhaps with the teacher's assistance, the important questions relating to self-esteem:

1. Does the child appear to have self-confidence? Verbal clues from the child will assist the parent in formulating an answer. Comments such as "I'm stupid," or "I can do that easily" indicate how the child feels about himself.
2. Is the child fearful of new experiences? The child who is hesitant to try the unknown indicates mistrust of his own abilities. A child who is afraid to make a mistake will not want to try the unknown since there is a chance for failure.
3. How does the child handle failure? Failure is inevitable in life and often an important part of the learning process. If the child seeks constant perfection, he excludes experiences which can lead to initial failure but also to eventual success.
4. Does the child continually boast or make up tales to enhance his status? The boastful child is often trying to compensate for weaknesses. Unfortunately, the untruths usually have an effect contrary to the desired one and cause a lack of trust by others.
5. Does the child have an unusually strong need for positive reinforcement? Constant need for encouragement and positive feedback is a help signal indicating a lack of confidence.
6. How does the child feel about his physical appearance? The child needs to be proud of his appearance since this is his most noticeable characteristic.
7. Is the child possessive of material objects? If the child does not relate well to other people, he can become overly concerned with inanimate objects and find security in material possessions. He will be extremely hesitant to share these possessions with others.
8. Does the child seek opportunities for independence? The desire to make decisions indicates a confidence in ability and a willingness to take responsibility.

9. Is the child permitted and willing to express his own ideas and opinions? A child indicates confidence in his own worth when he is willing to vocalize his thoughts.
10. How does the child handle responsibility? A willingness to accept increasing responsibility indicates continuing growth.

HELEN FELSENTHAL

Should a large percentage of our future citizens feel low self-worth, our country will be weakened. Studies show that the child with low self-esteem is less interested in public affairs (internal problems capture their attention). They are less likely to take part in public issues (they feel threatened by expressing opinions, doubt the value of their ideas, and are self-conscious about expressing themselves). They do not have the courage of their convictions. When you help children to high self-esteem, you take active steps to ensure that our democracy remains strong.

DOROTHY CORKILLE BRIGGS

Treat Friends, Kids the Same

On TV the other day, a leading child psychologist said parents should treat their children as they would treat their best friend . . . with courtesy, dignity and diplomacy.

"I have never treated my children any other way," I told myself. But later that night, I thought about it. Did I really talk to my best friends like I talked to my children? Just suppose . . . our good friends, Fred and Eleanor, came to dinner one night and . . . .

"Well, it's about time you two got here! What have you been doing? Dawdling? Leave those shoes outside, Fred. They've got mud on them. And shut the door. Were you born in a barn?

"So, Eleanor, how have you been? I've been meaning to have you over for such a long time. Fred! Take it easy on the chip dip or you'll ruin your dinner. I didn't work over a hot stove all day long to have you nibble like some bird.

"Heard from any of the gang lately? Got a card from the Martins. Yes, they're in Lauderdale again. They go every year to the same spot. What's the matter with you, Fred? You're fidgeting. Of course you have to go. It's down the hall, first door on the left. And I don't want to see a towel in the middle of the floor when you're finished.

"Did you wash your face before you came, Eleanor? I see a dark spot around your mouth. I guess it's a shadow. So, how're your children? If you ask me I think summer school is great for them. Is everybody hungry? then, why don't we go into dinner? You all wash up and I'll take up the food. Don't tell me your hands are clean, Eleanor. I saw you playing with the dog.

"Fred, you sit over there and Eleanor you can sit with the half glass of milk. You know you're all elbows when it comes to milk. There now, your host will say grace.

"Fred, I don't see any cauliflower on your plate. Have you ever tried it? Well, try a spoonful. If you don't like it I won't make you finish it, but if you don't try it, you can just forget dessert. And sit up straight or your spine will grow that way. Now, what were we talking about? Oh yes, the Gerbers. They sold their house. I mean they took a beating but . . . Eleanor, don't talk with food in your mouth. I can't understand a word you're saying. And use your napkin.

At that moment in my fantasy, my son walked into the room. "How nice of you to come," I said pleasantly.

"Now what did I do," he sighed.

ERMA BOMBECK

16

Your Students' Self-Ima

. . . even the most insensitive parent or teacher can usually recognize and take into account a crippling physical handicap. Negative self-esteem, however, is often overlooked because we fail to take the time and effort it requires to be sensitive to how children see themselves and their abilities.

WILLIAM W. PURKEY

Important for teachers is the fact that self-concepts are not unalterably fixed, but rather are modified by every life experience through at least the maturing years. Inherent in the thought that self-concept is learned as a function of experience is the fact that it can be taught. Interpersonal theory, then, holds that self-concept is built or achieved through accumulated social experiences and contacts.

WALLACE D. LA BENNE
BERT I. GREENE

The indications seem to be that success or failure in school significantly influences the ways in which students view themselves. Students who experience repeated success in school are likely to develop positive feelings about their abilities, while those who encounter failure tend to develop negative views of themselves. In the light of the influence of the self concept on academic achievement, it would seem like a good idea for schools to follow the precept I saw printed on an automobile drag-strip racing program: "Every effort is made to insure that each entry has a reasonable chance of victory."

WILLIAM W. PURKEY

A little child went to school and the teacher asked his name. He replied: "Johnny don't."

. . . whenever a value is set forth which can only be attained by a few, the conditions are ripe for widespread feelings of personal inadequacy. An outstanding example in American society is the fierce competitiveness of the school system. No educational system in the world has so many examinations, or so emphasized grades, as the American school system. Children are constantly being ranked and evaluated. The superior achievement of one child tends to debase the achievement of another.

MORRIS ROSENBERG

Students who misbehave generally have a negative self-regard. They may feel unwelcome, ugly, mean, unsuccessful, unimportant, or stupid. People tend to behave in ways consistent with their self-concept. In a class in which democratic discipline is established, the students help set the standards. Where students have a perception of shared objectives, a feeling of "we-ness" and cohesiveness is maintained. This cooperative action produces a common set of goals whereby each student feels he has a stake in the ongoing process of his education and classroom behavior.

WALLACE D. LA BENNE

Practices That Help Acceptance

To produce students who are able to accept themselves accurately and realistically, we need open, accepting school situations. This requires teachers, administrators, supervisors who are accepting of children as they are and who can treat them as persons of dignity and integrity. People learn acceptance from being accepted. Of primary importance in this task will be the kind of atmosphere we create, whether it be in the school as a whole or in some more limited place like a particular classroom, playing field, or laboratory.

From the time a student enters the campus, the school atmosphere needs to communicate acceptance. In such an atmosphere students need have no fear of being themselves. They should sense that they are accepted as persons by all around them. Students should be involved in formulating rules and regulations and thus will have no fear of such rules or desire to sabotage them. Students should be encouraged to be active without fear of making mistakes.

The relationship the teacher has with each individual pupil is crucial in establishing acceptance. It is not too hard to accept the "good" child and to be patient with his immaturity. However, accepting an actively misbehaving child who is constantly on the move may be much more difficult. Lecturing, punishing or coercing will certainly not result in self-acceptance; nor can the child see himself as being accepted when the teacher becomes a doormat. Teachers must learn how to deal with a misbehaving student in such a way that he comes to see himself as acceptable. The teacher's problem is to create a way of behaving which does not encourage the annoying behavior while at the same time maintaining a friendly, accepting atmosphere. This calls for ways of behaving that neither attack nor appease, but which recognize and respect the fundamental dignity and integrity of the individual.

ASSOCIATION FOR SUPERVISION AND CURRICULUM DEVELOPMENT

He always wanted to say things. But no one understood.
He always wanted to explain things. But no one cared.
So he drew.

Sometimes he would just draw and it wasn't anything. He wanted
to carve it in stone or write it in the sky.
He would lie out on the grass and look up in the sky and it would
be only him and the sky and the things inside that needed
saying.

And it was after that, that he drew the picture. It was a beautiful
picture. He kept it under the pillow and would let no one see it.
And he would look at it every night and think about it. And when
it was dark, and his eyes were closed, he could still see it.
And it was all of him. And he loved it.

When he started school he brought it with him. Not to show anyone, but just to have with him like a friend.

It was funny about school.
He sat in a square, brown desk like all the other square, brown
desks and he thought it should be red.
And his room was a square, brown room. Like all the other rooms.
And it was tight and close. And stiff.

He hated to hold the pencil and the chalk, with his arm stiff and
his feet flat on the floor, stiff, with the teacher watching
and watching.
And then he had to write numbers. And they weren't anything.
They were worse than the letters that could be something if
you put them together.
And the numbers were tight and square and he hated the whole
thing.

The teacher came and spoke to him. She told him to wear a tie like
all the other boys. He said he didn't like them and she said
it didn't matter.
After that they drew. And he drew all yellow and it was the way
he felt about morning. And it was beautiful.

The teacher came and smiled at him.
"What's this?" she said.
"Why don't you draw something like Ken's drawing?
Isn't that beautiful?"
It was all questions.

After that his mother bought him a tie and he always drew
airplanes and rocket ships like everyone else.
And he threw the old picture away.
And when he lay out alone looking at the sky, it was big and blue
and all of everything, but *he* wasn't anymore.

He was square inside and brown, and his hands were stiff, and he
was like anyone else. And the thing inside him that needed
saying didn't need saying anymore.

It had stopped pushing. It was crushed. Stiff.
Like everything else.

ANONYMOUS

. . . a senior turned this poem in to his teacher at a Regina,
Saskatchewan high school. The poem is labeled anonymous because the teacher isn't sure that the student wrote it. He has no
way to find out because a few weeks later the student committed
suicide.

MERRILL HARMIN
TOM GREGORY

Accept the Student As He Is

Educators have preached this sermon for so many years that it hardly requires to be repeated here. And yet, students have been so little accepted by teachers that we feel compelled to say it again. The process of encouragement demands that teachers accept the student as he is—with all his talents and faults, strengths and weaknesses. After all, we really have little choice in this matter. To do otherwise is to tell the student that we cannot accept him until he does as we say. To him, this means that we do not like him. If we who work closely with him do not like him as he is and cannot accept him, how can we expect him to like himself? We *must* accept him as we find him and try to help him become the kind of person he wants to be. In many cases, the person he wants to be is very similar to the person we would like him to be. When he knows that we accept him and that we have faith in his abilities, we are then in a position to have influence with him. Without this relationship, we cannot even communicate with him and are without influence. Students desperately want to be aided, assisted, and influenced by their teachers, but they do not want to be dominated by them.

WALLACE D. LA BENNE
BERT I. GREENE

The following are some suggestions useful in both the home and the classroom for helping a child attain a positive orientation to himself.

1. Realistically assess strengths and assist the child in becoming aware of his assets.
2. When it is necessary to correct or discipline a child, do so individually, never in front of others.
3. Call attention to a child's strengths not only individually but also before others.
4. Establish an environment in which the child is genuinely respected, in which he is heard, his ideas are tried, and he has opportunities to share in real responsibilities, not tasks created to keep him busy.
5. Establish a permissive atmosphere which encourages the shy and withdrawn child to participate and which gives him the freedom to express himself openly. The classroom environment should be under continual examination.
6. "Methods of developing feelings of adequacy in the child through encouragement, love, and guidance should be utilized at all levels, and particularly in the elementary school grades."
7. "Parents should be helped to recognize that each child is unique and functions in terms of his self concept. Ways to create better relationships between parents and children should be devised so that true understanding is promoted."
8. Avoid abnormally dependent relationships with one or two socially isolated children by integrating the child into a group. Accept him, but don't adopt him.
9. Group participation rather than individual exhibition of skills is important for the isolated child.
10. Look, nevertheless, for opportunities for the isolated child to help another successfully in a skill, game, or school subject.
11. With concern and consideration, evaluate the suggestions of class members in helping the isolated child toward better adjustment.

12. The development of at least one mutual friendship is exceedingly important. An equal relationship rather than an unequal, dependent one should be encouraged.

13. Solicit the help of the parents in developing friendships by suggesting that they include other children in family activities and trips.

14. Attempt to develop in the child a willingness to accept help from others.

15. Lastly and most important, a child's feelings for others are determined by his feelings toward self. Help him to accept and care for himself, his school work, and others.

WHITFIELD BOURISSEAU

The Little Boy

Once a little boy went to school.
He was quite a little boy.
And it was quite a big school.
But when the little boy
Found that he could go to his room
By walking right in from the door outside,
He was happy.
And the school did not seem
Quite so *big* any more.

One morning,
When the little boy had been in school awhile,
The teacher said:

"Today we are going to make a picture."
"Good!" thought the little boy.
He *liked* to make pictures.
He could make all kinds:
Lions and tigers,
Chickens and cows,
Trains and boats—.
And he took out his box of crayons
And began to draw.

But the teacher said: "Wait!
It is not time to begin!"
And she waited until everyone looked ready.

"Now," said the teacher,
"We are going to make flowers."
"Good!" thought the little boy,
He *liked* to make flowers,
And he began to make beautiful ones
With his pink and orange and blue crayons.

But the teacher said, "Wait!
And I will show you how."
And she drew a flower on the blackboard.
It was red, with a green stem.
"There," said the teacher.
"Now you may begin."

The little boy looked at the teacher's flower.
Then he looked at his own flower,
He liked *his* flower better than the teacher's.
But he did not say this,
He just turned his paper over
And made a flower like the teacher's.

It was red, with a green stem.

On another day,
When the little boy had opened
The door from the outside all by himself,
The teacher said:
"Today we are going to make something with clay."
"Good!" thought the little boy,
He *liked* clay.

He could make all kinds of things with clay:
Snakes and snowmen,
Elephants and mice,
Cars and trucks—
And he began to pull and pinch
His ball of clay.

But the teacher said,
"Wait! It is not time to begin!"
And she waited until everyone looked ready.

"Now," said the teacher,
"We are going to make a dish."
"Good!" thought the little boy,
He *liked* to make dishes,
And he began to make some
That were all shapes and sizes.

But the teacher said, "Wait!
And I will show you how."
And she showed everyone how to make
One deep dish.
"There," said the teacher,
"Now you may begin."

The little boy looked at the teacher's dish.
Then he looked at his own.
He *liked* his dishes better than the teacher's.
But he did not say this.
He just rolled his clay into a big ball again,
And made a dish like the teacher's.
It was a deep dish.

And pretty soon
The little boy learned to wait
And to watch,
And to make things just like the teacher.
And pretty soon
He didn't make things of his own anymore.

Then it happened
That the little boy and his family
Moved to another house,
In another city,
And the little boy
Had to go to another school.

This school was even Bigger
Than this other one,
And there was no door from the outside
Into his room.
He had to go up some big steps,
And walk down a long hall
To get to his room.

And the very first day
He was there,
The teacher said:
"Today we are going to make a picture."

"Good!" thought the little boy,
And he waited for the teacher
To tell him what to do.
But the teacher didn't say anything.
She just walked around the room.

When she came to the little boy
She said, "Don't you want to make a picture?"
"Yes," said the little boy,
"What are we going to make?"
"I don't know until you make it," said the teacher.
"*How* shall I make it?" asked the little boy.
"Why, any way you like," said the teacher.
"And any color?" asked the little boy.
"Any color," said the teacher,
"If everyone made the same picture,
And used the same colors,
How would I know who made what,
And which was which?"
"I don't know," said the little boy.
And he began to make pink and orange and blue flowers.

He liked his new school.
Even if it didn't have a door.
Right in from the outside!

HELEN E. BUCKLEY

Our Classroom Covenant

I have a right to be happy, and to be treated with
    kindness in this room;
    This means that no one
    Will laugh at me, ignore me, or
    Hurt my feelings.

I have a right to be myself in this room;
    This means that no one will
    Treat me unfairly because I am
    Fat or thin
    Fast or slow
    Boy or girl.

I have a right to be safe in this room;
    This means that no one will
    Hit me, Kick me
    push me, or pinch me.

I have a right to hear and be heard in this room;
    This means that no one will
    yell—scream—or shout
    And my opinions and desires will be considered
    In any plans we make.

I have a right to learn about myself in this room;
    This means that I will be
    Free to express my feelings
    And opinions without being
    Interrupted or punished.

17

Women and Self-Esteem

WOMEN AND SELF-ESTEEM

Many women, even very successful ones, don't fully believe in themselves. They don't respect themselves as much as they'd like to. They lack the kind of self-confidence that most of the men in their lives seem to take for granted.

Women are at greater risk of having low self-esteem, and a woman with low self-esteem tends to be more self-critical and more dependent. Her sense of her own competence is shaky. She may respond to difficulties by becoming depressed.

Low self-esteem goes back to our earliest relationships. Women who received unconditional positive regard as babies and young children tend to be much more self-confident. Those who didn't are more likely to think less of themselves. Unfortunately, even today, most prospective parents hope their child will be a boy. If you start life as a disappointment to one or both of your parents, you're less likely to feel you're totally acceptable.

In addition, many girls learn negative self-esteem from their mothers. Women are undervalued in our society, and housewives are the most undervalued of all. Their daughters may pick up these feelings of low self-worth.

Women with low self-esteem feel they have few inner resources, and must turn to others for emotional support and reassurance. They may need an almost constant supply of externally derived support to maintain their own precarious equilibrium.

Self-Care for Low Self-Esteem. There's no simple recipe for building self-esteem. The crux of the matter is that you need to stop settling for second best and go after what you really want. This means different things for different women, but here are a few guidelines that should be useful:

Spend time with supportive women friends, support groups, and consciousness-raising groups. These can be vital sources of encouragement. They allow women to come together as surrogate sisters, validating each other's feelings and beliefs.

Prepare yourself to earn your own living. A woman who knows that she could, if necessary, support herself is far less likely to put up with a destructive relationship.

Don't allow your man, husband, boyfriend, or partner to exploit or abuse you. Women with low self-esteem have a tendency to become involved in abusive relationships. You must absolutely commit yourself to stopping that. Taking this position will usually stop the abuse. If it continues, consult a family violence counselor, and be prepared to leave.

Spend time alone. Women need the opportunity to find out that they can make their world work for themselves. Even in a long-term relationship, it's important to have blocks of time to yourself.

Exercise regularly. Physical activity has given many women an enhanced sense of strength and self-worth. Consider taking a self-defense class. Feeling you're a powerful person enhances self-esteem.

Participate in a variety of cultural, physical, and community activities. If something goes wrong in one or two areas of your life, you have other options.

Make friends outside your family. Many women tend to depend too much on their partners.

Finally, seek out other people — women or men — with high self-esteem: friends who make you feel good about yourself, who care but also realize you can't please everyone; people with a variety of friends and a diversity of skills, who appreciate their strengths and feel at home in the world.

KAREN JOHNSON, M.D.

18

Self-Esteem and the Handicapped

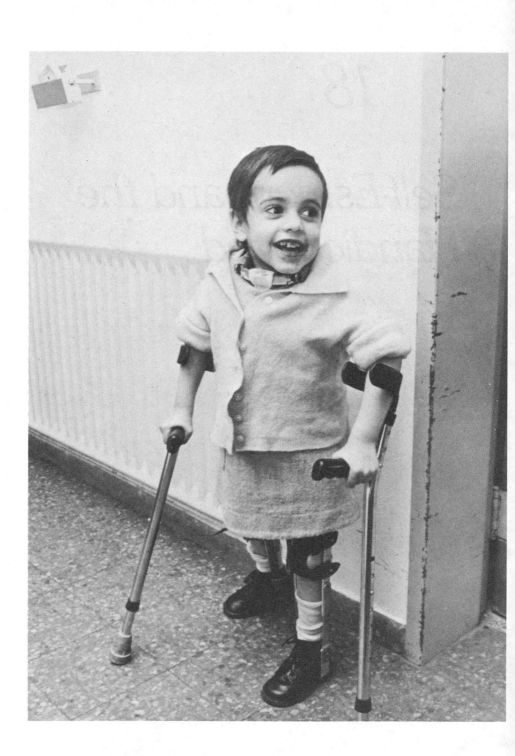

The "cripple" factor is most obvious in people with physical handicaps, but no one is immune to feeling inferior. Earlier I wrote about the eminently successful railway executive who felt that he was a zero, that he hadn't accomplished anything. And in my group therapy with the ministers I covered up the dark secret of my own handicap. You can imagine my amazement when I learned that everyone there had his own secret, a lifetime of heavy baggage that really weighed him down. That certainly made it easier for me to lighten my own burden.

The lesson hit home that a person's ultimate adjustment to a disability is closely related to his attitudes and values. I don't want to deny the fact that a disabled person does face many difficulties because of physical limitations and the real factors of environment. However, the disability is not as others see it as much as it is the disabled person's own perception.

If a person becomes crippled, his total functioning, his feelings of dignity and self-worth, are affected. His adjustment depends on the self-image he held before his accident or illness about the "whole body" — the perfect physique. If he insists on comparing himself to the intact person, he will always be imperfect in comparison and feel inferior, half a person. This is impoverished soil in which feelings of shame, guilt, embarrrassment, and worthlessness take root.

In his view, his social status is low and he may feel degraded because of his inferiority. His impotence is overwhelming. People regard him as a burden and feel that he cannot contribute his fair share. Girls won't want to go out with him. They will be repulsed by the sight of him. Now, that's how the disabled person often thinks people see him. And these feelings may be real or imagined.

Suppose you're a crippled person and that others really do have negative feelings about you. You can always find someone who will pity you or put you down as part of a minority or disadvantaged group. If you allow yourself to accept these outside valuations of yourself, you will doubt your own self-worth and this distorted viewpoint becomes a self-fulfilling prophecy.

As a result, you may become completely unaware of or won't even trust the fact that many people view you with the highest regard. They may see you as a brave and honorable person who has faced difficult circumstances, surmounted his handicap, and come out a beautiful human being. They may deeply admire you because, in a sense, they themselves are struggling with the same issues of self-worth that you are. And you may give them courage.

If you're disabled, there should come a time when you become cognizant of your strengths, drop any feelings of worthlessness, and say to yourself, "I am a whole person despite my handicap." Take onto yourself the viewpoints of those who look up to you. The most successful people are those in every walk of life who know who they are, accept who they are, and live who they are.

If a handicapped person idealizes the "normal" standards, he relegates himself to a permanent inferior position. To forget and conceal his disability, he must act as if he were not different from others. Such unrealistic behavior only reinforces feelings of guilt and inferiority.

The cycle spirals. Attempting to escape inferior feelings, such a person competes as if he had no handicap, inevitably fails, and becomes increasingly resentful of an unjust world. The harder he struggles, the more he is rejected by the "normal" society. He remains the marginal man, belonging to neither one group nor the other. Until he accepts himself as he is, he will not achieve identity integration.

In the real world, a person who becomes seriously ill or physically disabled is forced to be somewhat dependent, even if only temporarily. However, if he is seriously crippled, he must learn to accept a degree of lifelong dependency in some respects.

That's not an easy thing to do. Some people often deny their need for help in order to maintain their precious image of independence. If a person hides his dependency needs and pushes himself to the limits of his ability and endurance, he may progress outwardly but pay a high price in maladjustment.

Fortunately, there are powerful forces pushing the disabled person to take an active part in making the appropriate adjustment. Reality factors of ongoing life, work, community, family, and recreation drive him to accept his disability and accept himself as he is. The strain of hiding may exact too high and painful a cost of psychic energy.

I believe motivation is the key factor in overcoming a handicap. In my experience, patients who are strongly motivated to get better frequently improve remarkably despite severe physical handicaps, whereas mildly disabled patients who consider themselves as hopeless invalids may remain that way for the rest of their lives.

If a person attempts to "compensate" for his loss by emphasizing some other attributes, he frequently finds himself on a dead-end road. Seen in the perspective of asset values, a disabled person has nothing to compensate or make up for. He need have no shame or guilt. However, value changes are sometimes appropriate. A person who turns to painting because of a heart condition may find that art has a significant value, too — and a person's worth is not connected with his physique.

I know from my own experience that a disabled person is on the rewarding road to self-fulfillment when he accepts his handicap and no longer compares himself to the non-injured as the wished-for ideal. Once you realize that you have a self-image that is dragging you down, you can discard that excess baggage, concentrate on your positive and creative aspects, and express your specialness. If you recognize your own asset values, you won't seek artificial means, such as drugs, to sustain you. Just being yourself and opening yourself to the wonders and opportunities of this life will be fulfilling.

That's when you move out of the suffocating perspective, narrow and bleak, that all is lost, nothing is left, to the fresh air and wider perspective that life holds many possibilities and surprises. Your loss then becomes a dab of paint on a broad canvas of colors, varied and rich, that depict a person's whole life.

Every human being has certain aspects of his life that touch other human beings. We want to feel that we are worthwhile, that we do count, that we have dignity and a sense of responsibility. We are all subject to events and environments that we didn't create. And everything depends on how we respond to them, how we interpret them, and whether we are submerged by them or surmount them. If we can go beyond them, we can use the most difficult circumstances as rungs on a ladder, in a sense, heavenward.

PESACH KRAUSS

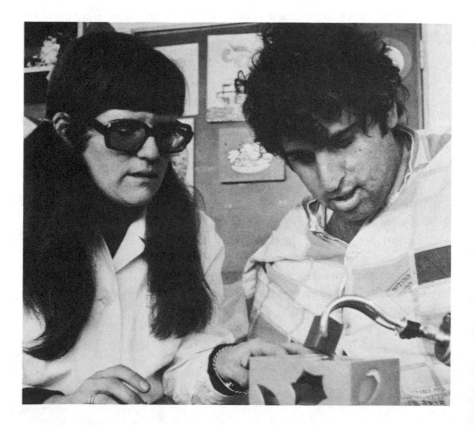

150

19

Spirituality and Self-Esteem

I do not believe it is possible to love someone else if you do not love yourself. Mother Theresa is coming, I assume, from a good strong ego position. And Christ said that you have to find your life before you can lose it. I absolutely believe that once you find the river in your own life, then you have to surrender to your own current. But one of the problems people have is that they are not willing to spend time. They feel they are being selfish. Often children grow up trying to please the parent, the teacher, society, and they never ask themselves, "Who am I?" Never. Their life begins to mean nothing because they're living in terms of pleasing, rather than in terms of being who they are. Until you know who you are, you cannot love another person. Until you are strong, you cannot surrender. It takes great spiritual flexibility to surrender.

MARION WOODMAN

ANAVA (humility, modesty) is a virtue attributed to Moses, father of the prophets (Nu. 12:13): "Moses was very modest ("anav"), more so than any human being on the face of the earth." The "anav" is modest, not meek; humble, not timid, a person who does not lack in self-esteem, but neither lusts for self-glorification. Being confident and assertive, not shy or diffident, the "anav" is a person without arrogance; well aware of his worth and virtues, he has no need to boast.

Genuine "anava" stems from a person's self-respect and sense of duty: He demands and expects much of himself; not bedazzled by his merits and achievements, he is able to face them with humility. From *Rabbinic Ethics* (Avot 2:9) "If you have learned much Torah, do not pride yourself; for this purpose you have been created."

RABBI ZVI YEHUDA

Bernard of Clairvaux, a great statesman of the twelfth-century church in France and master of the inner way, saw four stages of love as the milestones of spiritual growth:

First,   Loving self for self's sake
Second,   Loving God for self's sake
Third,   Loving God for God's sake
Fourth,   Loving self for God's sake

Praying with longing love marks the third stage: loving God for God's sake. A great leap occurs between stages two and three, from loving God for the sake of your security, your belonging, your self-esteem, and your spiritual self-development, to loving God for God's sake. In response to God's unconditional love a transformation of will and selfhood takes place.

EDWARD E. THORNTON

In the history of spirituality since the time of the Fathers, it has been common to distinguish three principal degrees in the spiritual life: the purgative, the illuminative, and the unitive...

Let me begin with a contemporary perspective on the purgative stage, bringing to bear upon our traditional understanding some insights from psychology. To "purge" means literally "to cleanse" and, in a spiritual sense, to cleanse from sin. If we might speak of sin as the failure to be our true selves, the children of God, we can discuss purgation as a getting rid of, a washing away of our untrue or false selves. In psychology, we might use the term "mask" or "facade" to connote an inauthentic or deceitful persona. I would like to think of the " purgative" stage as cleansing oneself from a false sense of self, particularly from low self-esteem. This perspective comprises the major component of doing spiritual direction with adolescents.

The teenager who desires a deeper relationship with the Lord must begin by purging himself or herself of earlier self concepts and self-image. St. Bernard of Clairvaux in his treatise on "The Love of God," asserts that the first stage in loving God is to develop a healthy self-love, an appreciation of our individual uniqueness in this world. Jesus himself points out to us that we should love one another as we have already been loved by him (Jn 15:12). One theological perspective on original sin is that its result is the inability to truly believe that we are totally loved by God. Jesus is the only person who possessed a perfect self image because he believed that the Father loved and accepted him completely...

Low self-esteem is the basis of so many adolescent issues including spiritual ones. There is research to indicate that if persons feel unloved and unworthy, they will also feel that God doesn't care much about them and certainly doesn't answer *their* prayer.

JOSEPH MOORE

Love of self according to spiritual and psychological teaching means not love your own Ego, which is exclusive love. Rather love your Higher self, within, which is inclusive love.

YOGI AMRIT DESAI

Before one prays for the redemption of the world, one must pray for his own redemption.

RABBI ISRAEL BAAL SHEM TOV

Yet before we can surrender ourselves we must become ourselves. For no one can give up what he does not possess.

THOMAS MERTON

The first half of life is to find ego. The second half is to relinquish it.

CARL G. JUNG

The spritual journey, as I understand it, is one of surrendering ego as the center, or determiner, in one's life. We come to know, after many initiations, that some larger unifying Force is guiding and providing. However, I cannot emphasize strongly enough, that one must possess a solid ego before it can be relinquished. You can't give up what you don't have.

SHEILA FOSTER

Both the Hebrew and Christian Scriptures command us to love the Lord our God with all our heart, and with all our soul, and with all our mind. Then we are commanded to love our neighbor *as* ourselves.

As ourselves. Not *more* than ourselves because that is impossible. We are no help to others if we are not appropriately attentive to ourselves. Commercial airlines are very aware of that. (Listen to the flight attendant telling "those travelling with small children" to adjust, if needed, the oxygen mask on themselves first, then on the small child.)

You and I are each someone unique. We are literally different from everyone else in this world. We are human and share the kind of being we are. We have other things in common with many other people: nationality, religion, race, sex. Still, each of us is unique. No one has my exact history, my exact experiences, actions, and reactions. There's not another person in this world who has my network of relations, friends, acquaintances, and not-so-much-liked people. And every one of us, made by God with infinite prodigality, is "very good," as the first book of the Bible says. It's important I come to know myself, my goodness. To love myself. To acknowledge in me the goodness of God's creation. Then I am able to know others, to acknowledge the goodness of God's creation in others, to love others.

SISTER MARLENE HALPIN, DOMINICAN

156

Recommended Reading

REYNOLD BEAN & HARRIS CLEMES, *Raising Children's Self Esteem*. Assoc. for Personal & Organizational Development, 1427 41st Avenue, Capitola, CA 95010.

REYNOLD BEAN & HARRIS CLEMES, *The Four Conditions of Self Esteem*. Assoc. for Personal & Organizational Development, 1427 41st Avenue, Capitola, CA 95010.

ROBERT A. BLUME, "How the Child Sees Himself May Relate to How the Teacher Sees Himself." *Michigan Education Journal*, 46:9-11, November, 1968.

NATHANIEL BRANDEN, *The Psychology of Self-Esteem*. Bantam Books, 1971.

DOROTHY C. BRIGGS, *Your Child's Self-Esteem*. Doubleday, 1970.

GAY BRYANT & BOCKRIS-WYLE, *How I Learned to Like Myself*. Warner Paperback, 1975.

JACK CANFIELD *Self-Esteem in the Classroom*, Self-Esteem Seminars, 17156 Palisades Circle, Pacific Palisades, CA 90272.

JACK CANFIELD & HAROLD C. WELLS, *One Hundred Ways to Enhance Self-Concept in the Classroom*. Prentice-Hall, 1975.

JACK CANFIELD & HAROLD C. WELLS, *About Me*. Student Book and Teachers Guide. Encyclopaedia Britannica Ed. Corp., 1971.

AMINAH CLARK, HARRIS CLEMES, REYNOLD BEAN, *Raising Teenager's Self Esteem*. Assoc. for Personal & Organizational Development, 1427 41st Avenue, Capitola, CA 95010.

STANLEY COOPERSMITH, *The Antecedents of Self-Esteem*. W. H. Freeman, 1967.

STANLEY COOPERSMITH, "Studies in Self-Esteem." *Scientific American*, February, 1968, pp. 96-106.

JAMES DOBSON, *Hide or Seek — Self-Esteem for the Child*. Revell, 1974.

DOV PERETZ ELKINS *Teaching People To Love Themselves: A Leader's Handbook of Theory & Technique For Self Esteem and Affirmation Training*. Rochester, NY: Growth Associates, 1978.

DOV PERETZ ELKINS *Self Concept Sourcebook: Ideas and Activities for Building Self-Esteem*. Rochester, NY: Growth Associates, 1978.

DOV PERETZ ELKINS *Twelve Pathways to Feeling Better About Yourself*. Rochester, NY: Growth Associates, 1978.

ERICH FROMM, "Selfishness, Self-Love and Self-Interest," *Man for Himself*. Holt, Rinehart & Winston, 1947, pp. 119-40.

JOHN V. GILMORE, *The Productive Personality*. Albion, 1974.

HAIM G. GINOTT, *Between Parent and Child*. Avon Books, 1969.

HAIM G. GINOTT, *Between Parent and Teenager.* Avon Books, 1971.

HAIM G. GINOTT, *Teacher and Child.* Avon Books, 1972.

THOMAS GORDON, *Parent Effectiveness Training.* Wyden, 1970.

THOMAS GORDON, *Teacher Effectiveness Training.* Wyden, 1974.

DON E. HAMACHEK, *Encounters with the Self.* Holt, Rinehart & Winston, 1971.

THOMAS A. HARRIS, *I'm OK, You're OK.* Harper & Row, 1967.

DAVID W. JOHNSON, *Reaching Out — Interpersonal Effectiveness & Self-Actualization.* Prentice-Hall, 1972.

WALLACE D. LABENNE & BERT I. GREEN, *Educational Implications of Self-Concept Theory.* Goodyear, 1969.

MAXWELL MALTZ, *The Magic Power of Self-Image Psychology.* Pocket Books, 1970.

EDITH G. NEISSER, *The Roots of Self-Confidence.* SRA, 1970.

HOWARD M. NEWBURGER & MARJORIE LEE, *Winners and Losers; Self-Image Modification.* David McKay, 1974.

MILDRED NEWMAN & BERNARD BERKOWITZ, *How to Be Your Own Best Friend.* Random House, 1971.

WILLIAM W. PURKEY, *Self Concept and School Achievement.* Prentice-Hall, 1970.

AYN RAND, *The Virtue of Selfishness: A New Concept of Egoism.* Signet, 1964.

CARL R. ROGERS, *On Becoming a Person.* Houghton Mifflin, 1961.

MORRIS ROSENBERG, *Society and the Adolescent Self-Image.* Princeton University, 1965.

THEODORE I. RUBIN, *Dr. Rubin, Please Make Me Happy.* Bantam, 1974.

W. RAY RUCKER et al, "Enhancement of the Self-Image by Teachers and Students," *Human Values in Education.* Kendall/Hunt, 1969.

VIRGINIA SATIR, *Peoplemaking.* Science and Behavior Books, 1972.

LOUIS M. SAVARY & PATRICIA H. BERNE, *Building Self-Esteem In Children.* NY: Continuum, 1987.

LORENE A. STRINGER, *The Sense of Self — A Guide to How We Mature.* Temple University Press, 1971.

BILL & CAROLE TEGELER, *The People Press — Life-Script Awareness.* University Associates, 1975.

PAUL TILLICH, *The Courage to Be.* Yale University Press, 1959.

RUTH C. WYLIE, *The Self-Concept.* University of Nebraska Press, 1961.

KAORU YAMAMOTO (ed.), *The Child and His Image — Self Concept in the Early Years.* Houghton Mifflin, 1972.

Photographs courtesy of the
Lewischam-Bethel Agency:

Photographs by Dov Peretz Elkins:

ORDER FORM

GROWTH ASSOCIATES
HUMAN RELATIONS CONSULTANTS & PUBLISHERS
P.O. BOX 18429, ROCHESTER, NEW YORK 14618-0429
(716) 244-1225

name _____
organization _____ position _____
street _____
city _____ state _____ zip _____

EDUCATIONAL MATERIALS BY DR. DOV PERETZ ELKINS

QTY.	DESCRIPTION	PRICE
	My Seventy-Two Friends: Encounters with Refuseniks in the U.S.S.R. **$12.** *NEW*	
	Experiential Programs for Jewish Groups: Thirty full-length programs **$10.**	
	Clarifying Jewish Values: 25 Values Activities for Jewish Groups **$10.**	
	Jewish Consciousness Raising: 50 Experiential Exercises **$10.**	
	Loving My Jewishness: Jewish Self-Pride & Self-Esteem. A text for adult & teenage groups **$10.** Ten or more copies at $5 each, including Leader's Guide.	
	Teaching People to Love Themselves: A Leader's Handbook of Theory & Technique for Self-Esteem Training -- includes 50 experiential exercises. Best seller. **$22**	
	Glad To Be Me: Building Self-Esteem in Yourself & Others **$12.** 1989 Rev. & Expanded Edition. *NEW*	
	Twelve Pathways to Feeling Better About Yourself: **$7.50.**	
	Self Concept Source Book: Ideas & Activites for Building Self-Esteem **$19.**	
	The Ideal Jew: A Value Clarification Program (Leader's Guide & 15 participants' forms) **$6 per set.**	
	"New Age Judaism" --Packet of articles & lectures on the theory & practice of Experiential Learning written since Humanizing Jewish Life **$4.**	
	Why Did Susan Cohen Desert Judaism? A Value Clarification Program on Intermarriage, Assimilation, Jewish Community Priorities (Leader's Guide & 15 participant's forms). **$6 per set.**	
	Shepherd of Jerusalem: A Biography of Chief Rabbi Abraham Isaac Kook **$10**	
	Worlds Lost and Found: Discoveries in Biblical Archeology (with Azriel Eisenberg). **$12.** Winner of Jewish Book Council Prize	Out of Print
	God's Warriors: Dramatic Adventures of Rabbis in Uniform **$10.00**	
	Rejoice With Jerusalem: Prayers, Readings & Songs for Israel Observances **$3.**	
	The Tallit: Some Modern Meanings (Jewish Tract Series) **$2.**	

All orders must be prepaid
Postage & Handling: $1.00 first book, $.50 each additional
Make checks payable to Growth Associates (US Funds please)

Subtotal
NY residents add 7% sales tax
TOTAL ORDER

Check here if interested in information on lectures, workshops, retreats and/or other training events _____

ORDER FORM

GROWTH ASSOCIATES
HUMAN RELATIONS CONSULTANTS & PUBLISHERS
P.O. BOX 18429, ROCHESTER, NEW YORK 14618-0429
(716) 244-1225

name _____

organization _____ position _____

street _____

city _____ state _____ zip _____

EDUCATIONAL MATERIALS BY DR. DOV PERETZ ELKINS

QTY.	DESCRIPTION	PRICE
	My Seventy-Two Friends: Encounters with Refuseniks in the U.S.S.R. **$12.** *NEW*	
	Experiential Programs for Jewish Groups: Thirty full-length programs **$10.**	
	Clarifying Jewish Values: 25 Values Activities for Jewish Groups **$10.**	
	Jewish Consciousness Raising: 50 Experiential Exercises **$10.**	
	Loving My Jewishness: Jewish Self-Pride & Self-Esteem. A text for adult & teenage groups **$10.** Ten or more copies at $5 each, including Leader's Guide.	
	Teaching People to Love Themselves: A Leader's Handbook of Theory & Technique for Self-Esteem Training -- includes 50 experiential exercises. <u>Best seller.</u> **$22**	
	Glad To Be Me: Building Self-Esteem in Yourself & Others **$12.** 1989 Rev. & Expanded Edition. *NEW*	
	Twelve Pathways to Feeling Better About Yourself: **$7.50.**	
	Self Concept Source Book: Ideas & Activites for Building Self-Esteem **$19.**	
	The Ideal Jew: A Value Clarification Program (Leader's Guide & 15 participants' forms) **$6 per set.**	
	"New Age Judaism" --Packet of articles & lectures on the theory & practice of Experiential Learning written since Humanizing Jewish Life **$4.**	
	Why Did Susan Cohen Desert Judaism? A Value Clarification Program on Intermarriage, Assimilation, Jewish Community Priorities (Leader's Guide & 15 participant's forms). **$6 per set.**	
	Shepherd of Jerusalem: A Biography of Chief Rabbi Abraham Isaac Kook **$10**	
	Worlds Lost and Found: Discoveries in Biblical Archeology (with Azriel Eisenberg). **$12.** Winner of Jewish Book Council Prize	Out of Print
	God's Warriors: Dramatic Adventures of Rabbis in Uniform **$10.00**	
	Rejoice With Jerusalem: Prayers, Readings & Songs for Israel Observances **$3.**	
	The Tallit: Some Modern Meanings (Jewish Tract Series) **$2.**	

All orders must be prepaid
Postage & Handling: $1.00 first book, $.50 each additional
Make checks payable to Growth Associates (US Funds please)

Subtotal
NY residents add 7% sales tax
TOTAL ORDER

Check here if interested in information on lectures, workshops, retreats and/or other training events _____

ORDER FORM

GROWTH ASSOCIATES
HUMAN RELATIONS CONSULTANTS & PUBLISHERS
P.O. BOX 18429, ROCHESTER, NEW YORK 14618-0429
(716) 244-1225

name _____

organization _____ position _____

street _____

city _____ state _____ zip _____

EDUCATIONAL MATERIALS BY DR. DOV PERETZ ELKINS

QTY	DESCRIPTION	PRICE
	My Seventy-Two Friends: Encounters with Refuseniks in the U.S.S.R. **$12.** *NEW*	
	Experiential Programs for Jewish Groups: Thirty full-length programs **$10.**	
	Clarifying Jewish Values: 25 Values Activities for Jewish Groups **$10.**	
	Jewish Consciousness Raising: 50 Experiential Exercises **$10.**	
	Loving My Jewishness: Jewish Self-Pride & Self-Esteem. A text for adult & teenage groups **$10.** Ten or more copies at $5 each, including Leader's Guide.	
	Teaching People to Love Themselves: A Leader's Handbook of Theory & Technique for Self-Esteem Training -- includes 50 experiential exercises. <u>Best seller</u>. **$22**	
	Glad To Be Me: Building Self-Esteem in Yourself & Others **$12.** 1989 Rev. & Expanded Edition. *NEW*	
	Twelve Pathways to Feeling Better About Yourself: **$7.50.**	
	Self Concept Source Book: Ideas & Activites for Building Self-Esteem **$19.**	
	The Ideal Jew: A Value Clarification Program (Leader's Guide & 15 participants' forms) **$6 per set.**	
	"New Age Judaism" --Packet of articles & lectures on the theory & practice of Experiential Learning written since Humanizing Jewish Life **$4.**	
	Why Did Susan Cohen Desert Judaism? A Value Clarification Program on Intermarriage, Assimilation, Jewish Community Priorities (Leader's Guide & 15 participant's forms). **$6 per set.**	
	Shepherd of Jerusalem: A Biography of Chief Rabbi Abraham Isaac Kook **$10**	
	Worlds Lost and Found: Discoveries in Biblical Archeology (with Azriel Eisenberg). **$12.** Winner of Jewish Book Council Prize	Out of Print
	God's Warriors: Dramatic Adventures of Rabbis in Uniform **$10.00**	
	Rejoice With Jerusalem: Prayers, Readings & Songs for Israel Observances **$3.**	
	The Tallit: Some Modern Meanings (Jewish Tract Series) **$2.**	

All orders must be prepaid
Postage & Handling: $1.00 first book, $.50 each additional
Make checks payable to Growth Associates (US Funds please)

Subtotal
NY residents add 7% sales tax
TOTAL ORDER

Check here if interested in information on lectures, workshops, retreats and/or other training events _____

ORDER
FORM

GROWTH ASSOCIATES
HUMAN RELATIONS CONSULTANTS & PUBLISHERS
P.O. BOX 18429, ROCHESTER, NEW YORK 14618-0429
(716) 244-1225

name _____

organization _____ position _____

street _____

city _____ state _____ zip _____

EDUCATIONAL MATERIALS BY DR. DOV PERETZ ELKINS

TY.	DESCRIPTION	PRICE
	My Seventy-Two Friends: Encounters with Refuseniks in the U.S.S.R. **$12.** *NEW*	
	Experiential Programs for Jewish Groups: Thirty full-length programs **$10.**	
	Clarifying Jewish Values: 25 Values Activities for Jewish Groups **$10.**	
	Jewish Consciousness Raising: 50 Experiential Exercises **$10.**	
	Loving My Jewishness: Jewish Self-Pride & Self-Esteem. A text for adult & teenage groups **$10.** Ten or more copies at $5 each, including Leader's Guide.	
	Teaching People to Love Themselves: A Leader's Handbook of Theory & Technique for Self-Esteem Training -- includes 50 experiential exercises. <u>Best seller</u>. **$22**	
	Glad To Be Me: Building Self-Esteem in Yourself & Others **$12.** 1989 Rev. & Expanded Edition. *NEW*	
	Twelve Pathways to Feeling Better About Yourself: $7.50.	
	Self Concept Source Book: Ideas & Activites for Building Self-Esteem **$19.**	
	The Ideal Jew: A Value Clarification Program (Leader's Guide & 15 participants' forms) **$6 per set.**	
	"New Age Judaism" --Packet of articles & lectures on the theory & practice of Experiential Learning written since Humanizing Jewish Life **$4.**	
	Why Did Susan Cohen Desert Judaism? A Value Clarification Program on Intermarriage, Assimilation, Jewish Community Priorities (Leader's Guide & 15 participant's forms). **$6 per set.**	
	Shepherd of Jerusalem: A Biography of Chief Rabbi Abraham Isaac Kook **$10**	
	Worlds Lost and Found: Discoveries in Biblical Archeology (with Azriel Eisenberg). **$12.** Winner of Jewish Book Council Prize	Out of Print
	God's Warriors: Dramatic Adventures of Rabbis in Uniform **$10.00**	
	Rejoice With Jerusalem: Prayers, Readings & Songs for Israel Observances **$3.**	
	The Tallit: Some Modern Meanings (Jewish Tract Series) **$2.**	

All orders must be prepaid
Postage & Handling: $1.00 first book, $.50 each additional
Make checks payable to Growth Associates (US Funds please)

Subtotal
NY residents add 7% sales tax
TOTAL ORDER

Check here if interested in information on lectures, workshops, retreats and/or other training events ____